IMAGES of FREMANTLE
by Brian Sanger

National Library of Australia Cataloguing-in-Publication entry

Creator: Sanger, Brian, 1939- author, photographer.
Title: Images of Fremantle / by Brian Sanger ;
                Compiled by David Solly Sandler,.
ISBN: 9780992468460 (paperback)
Series: Photographic art of Brian Sanger 2
Subjects: Sanger, Brian, 1939-
                Street photography--Western Australia--Fremantle.
                Photography, Artistic.
                Fremantle (W.A.)--Pictorial works.
Other Authors/Contributors:
                Sandler, David Solly, compiler.
Dewey Number: 779.4941

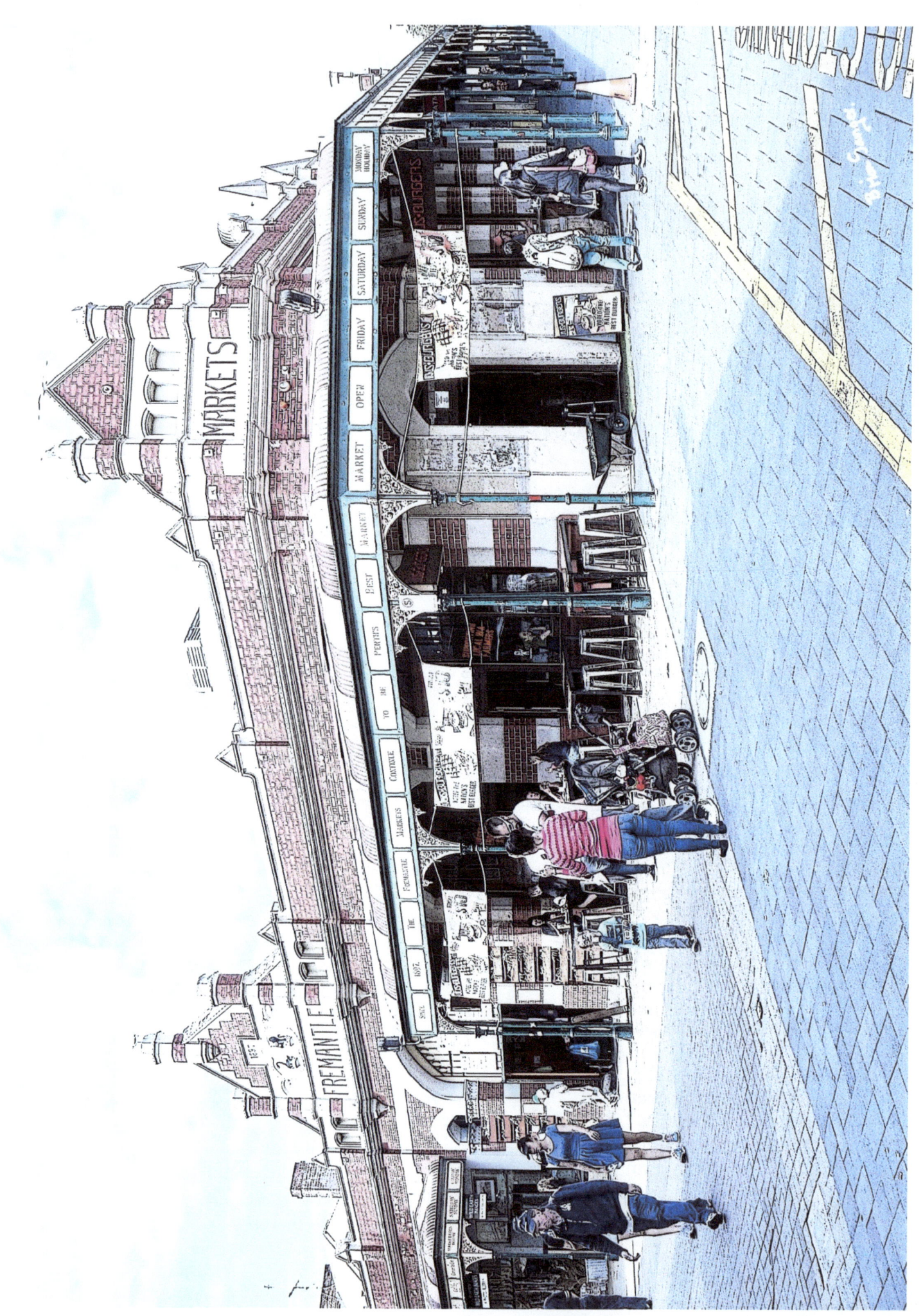

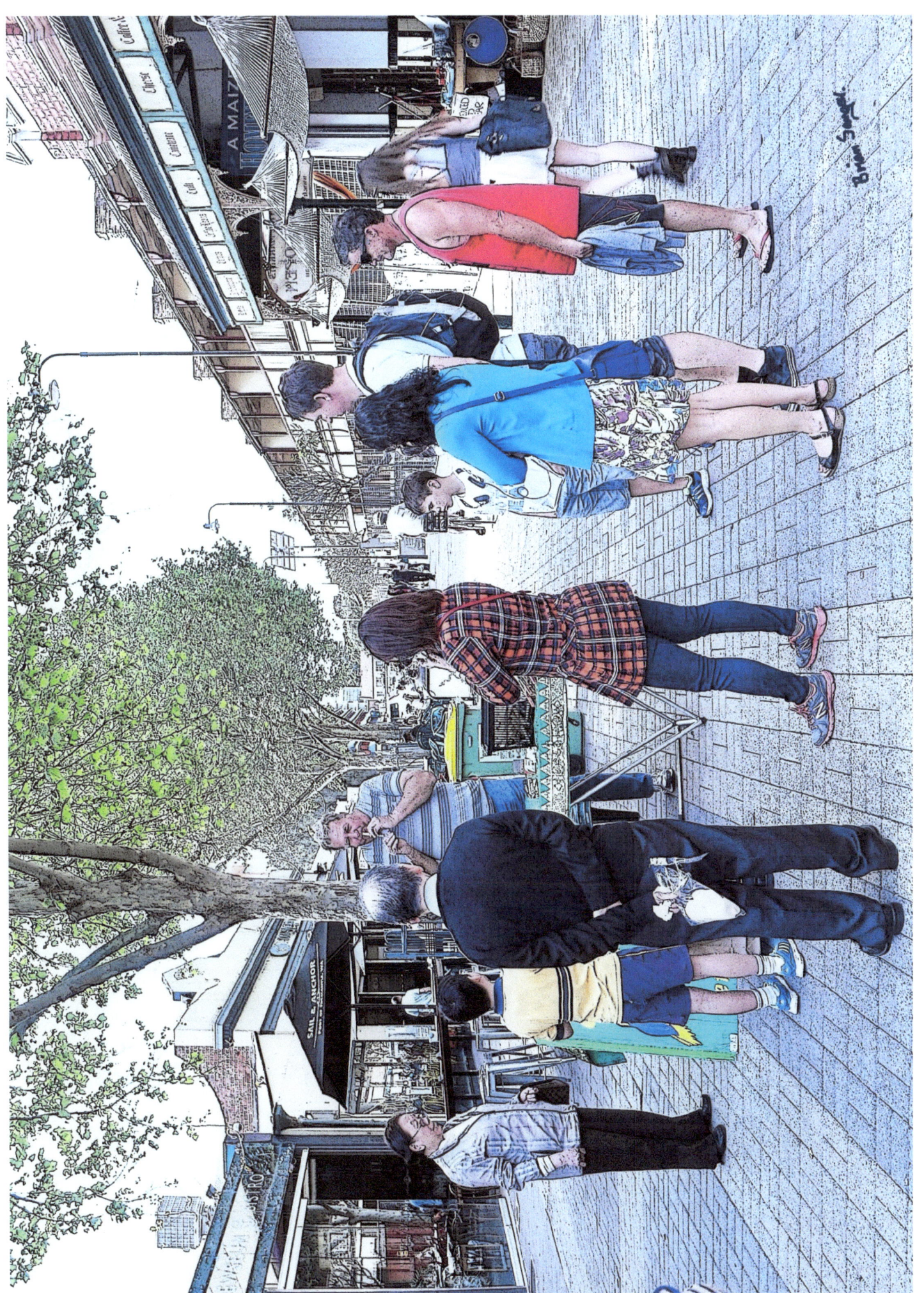

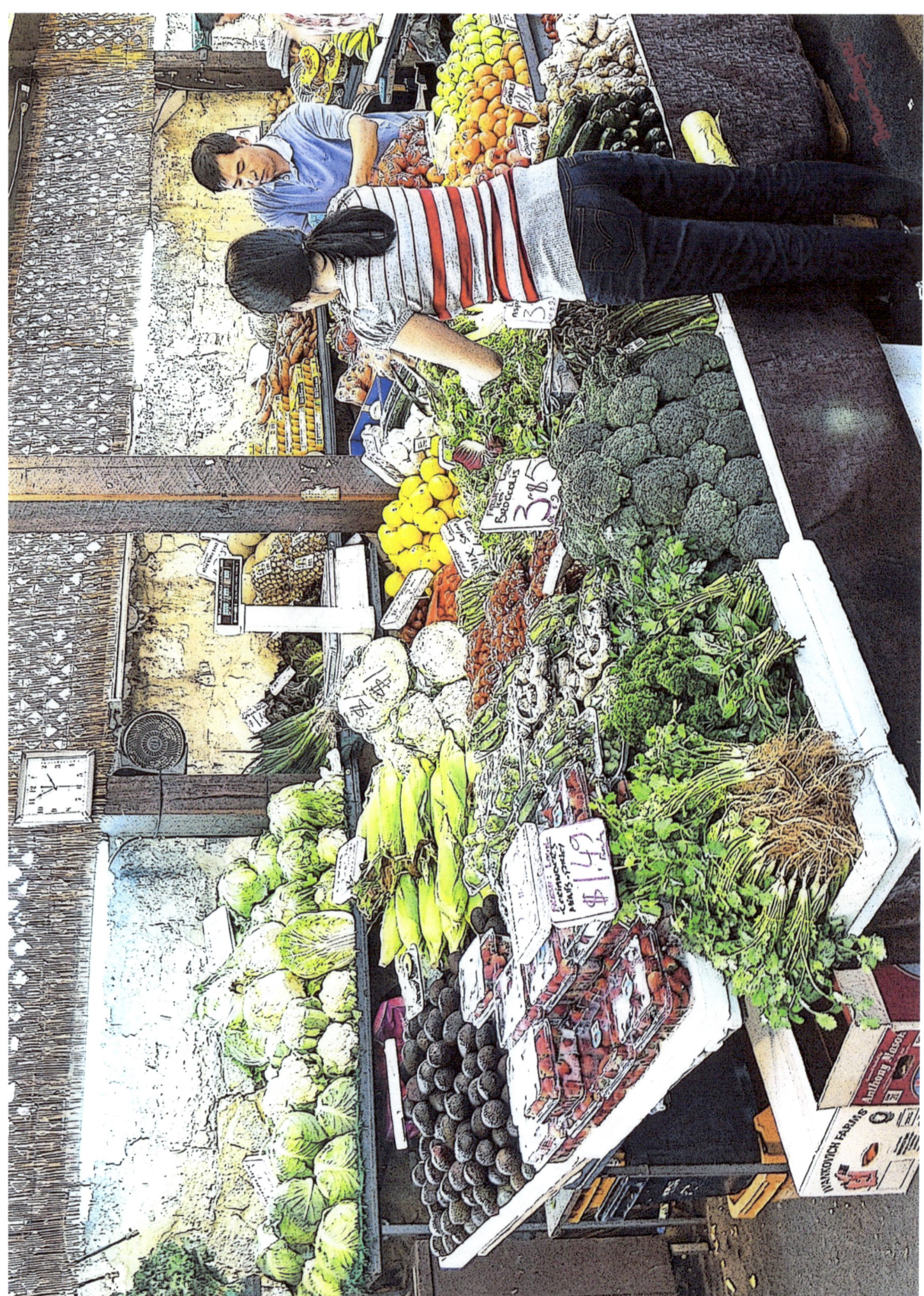

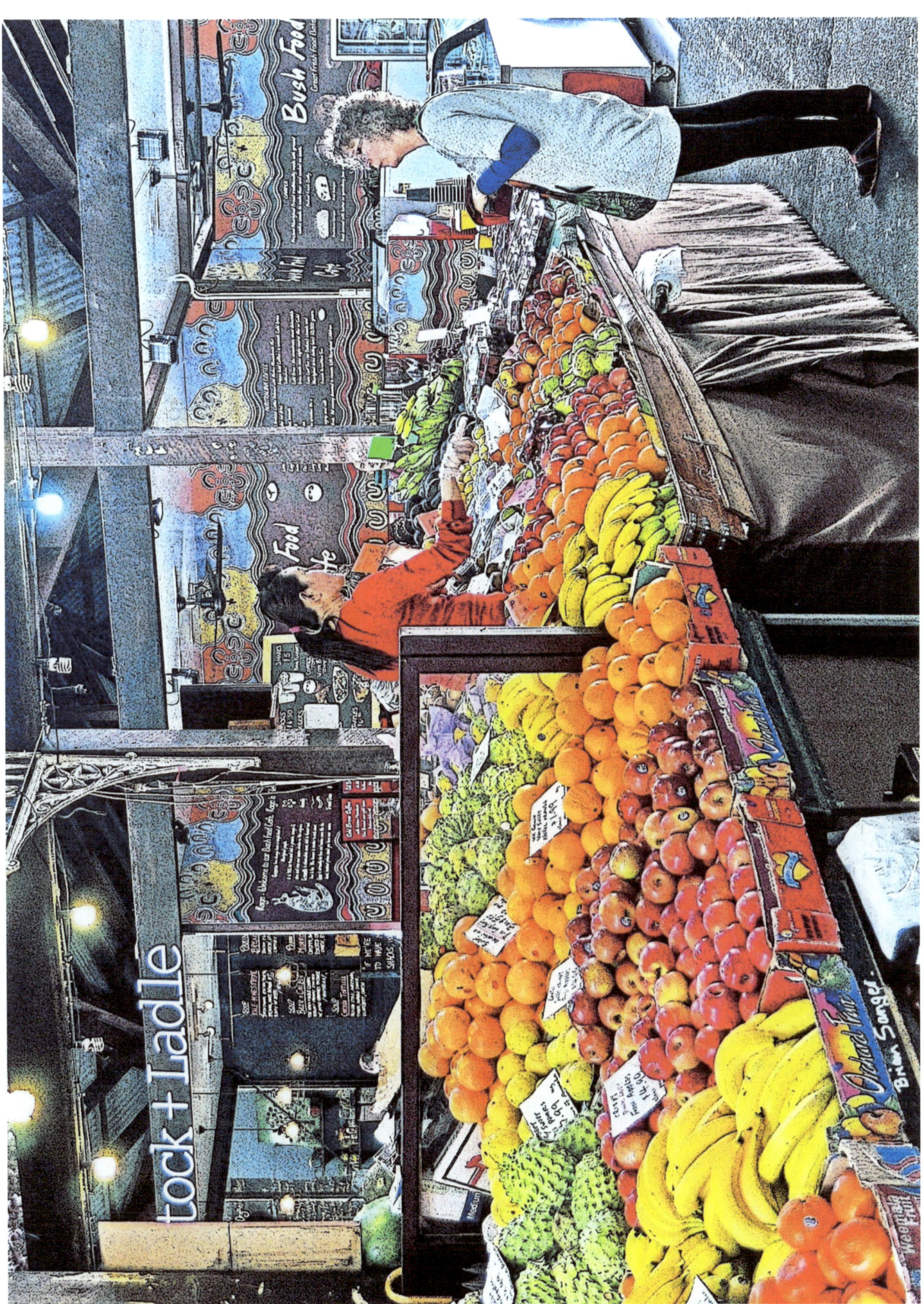

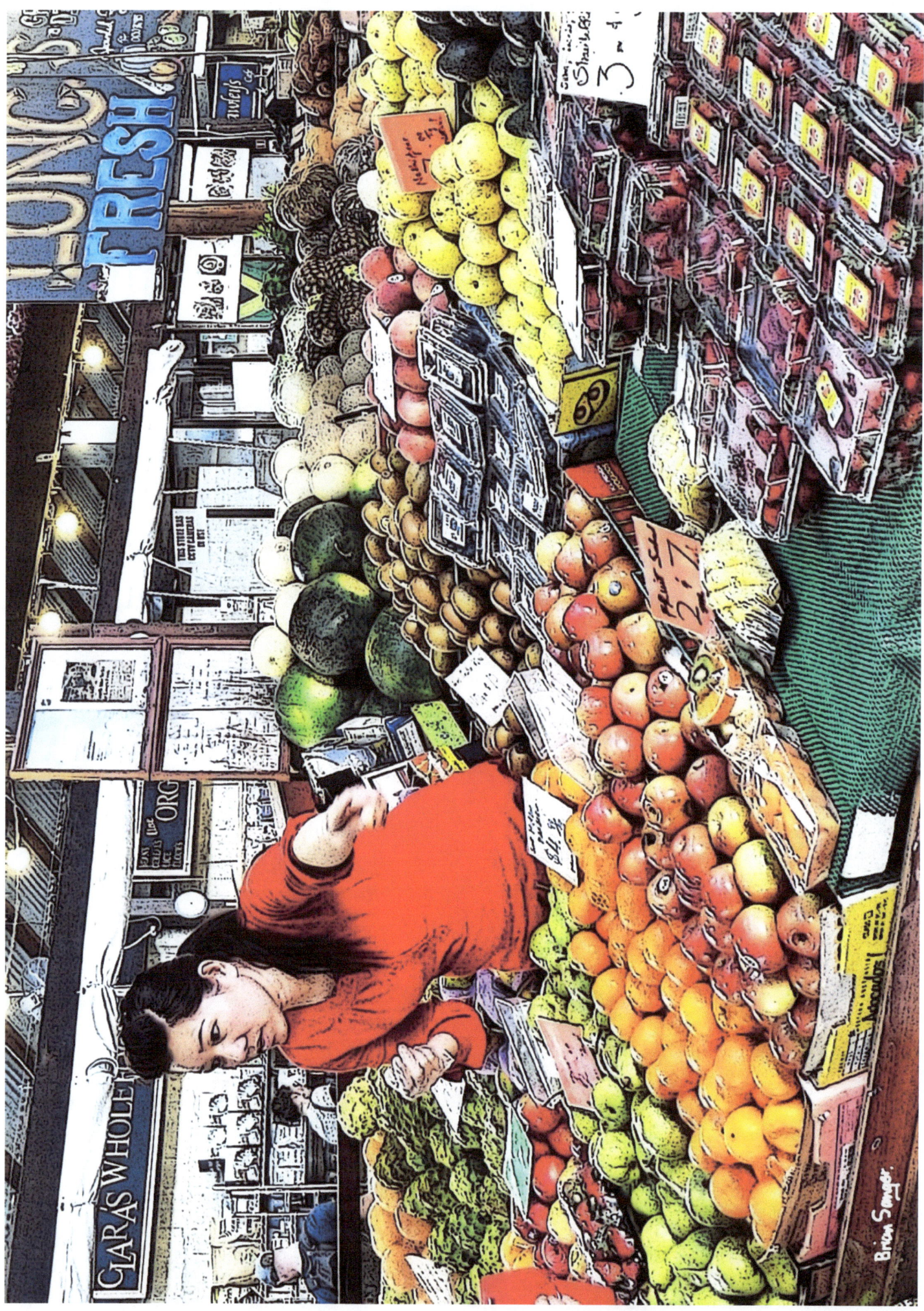

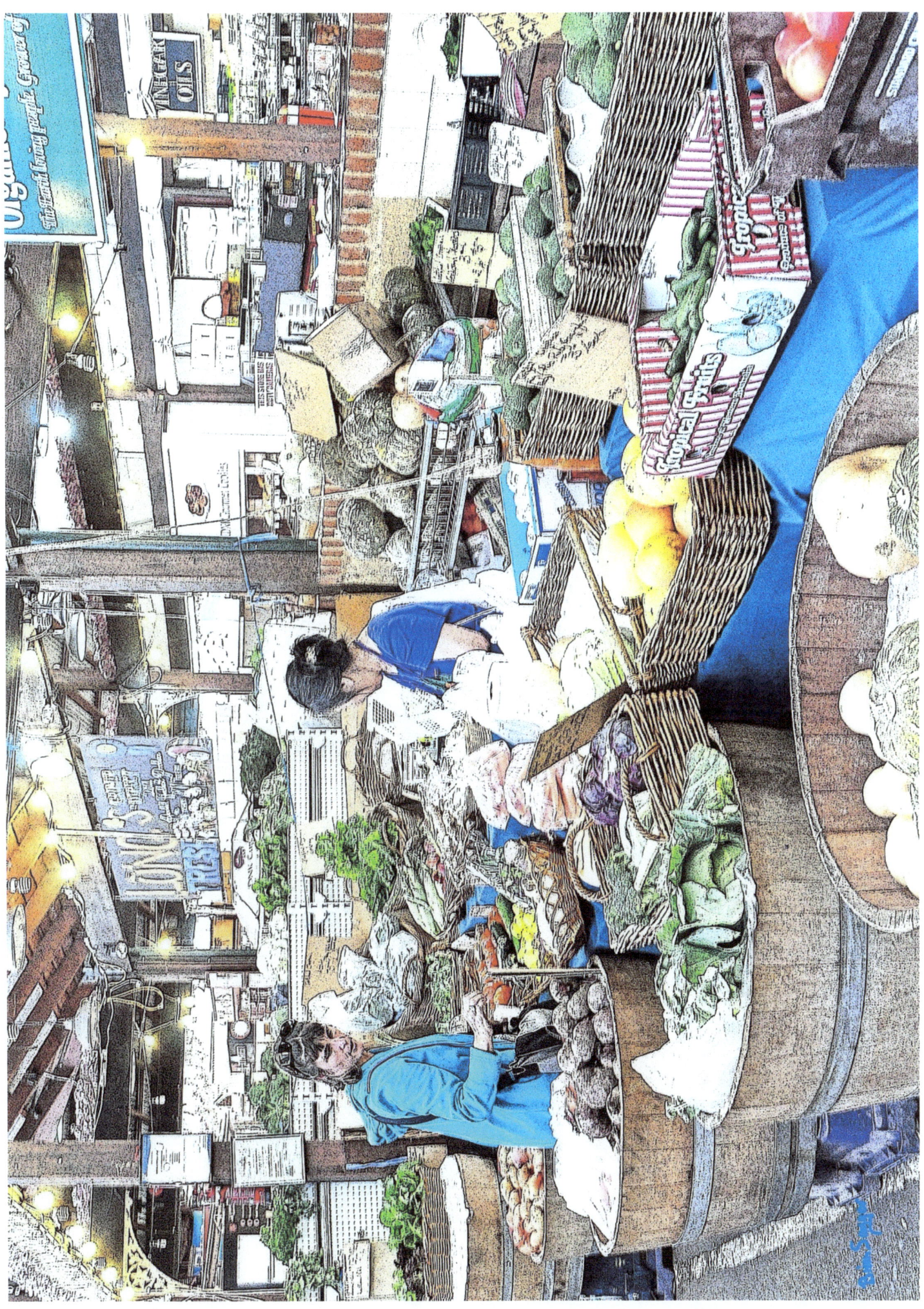

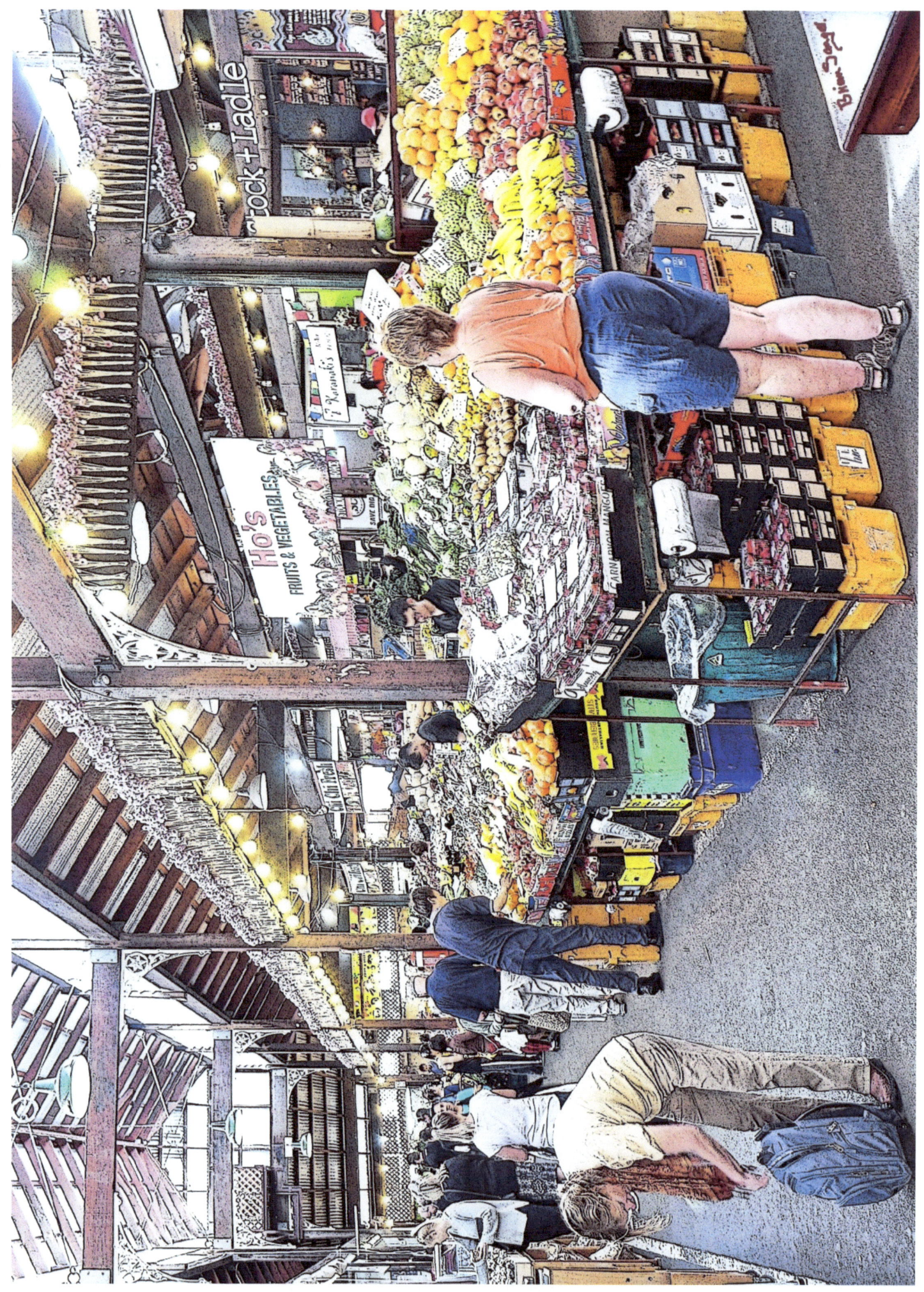

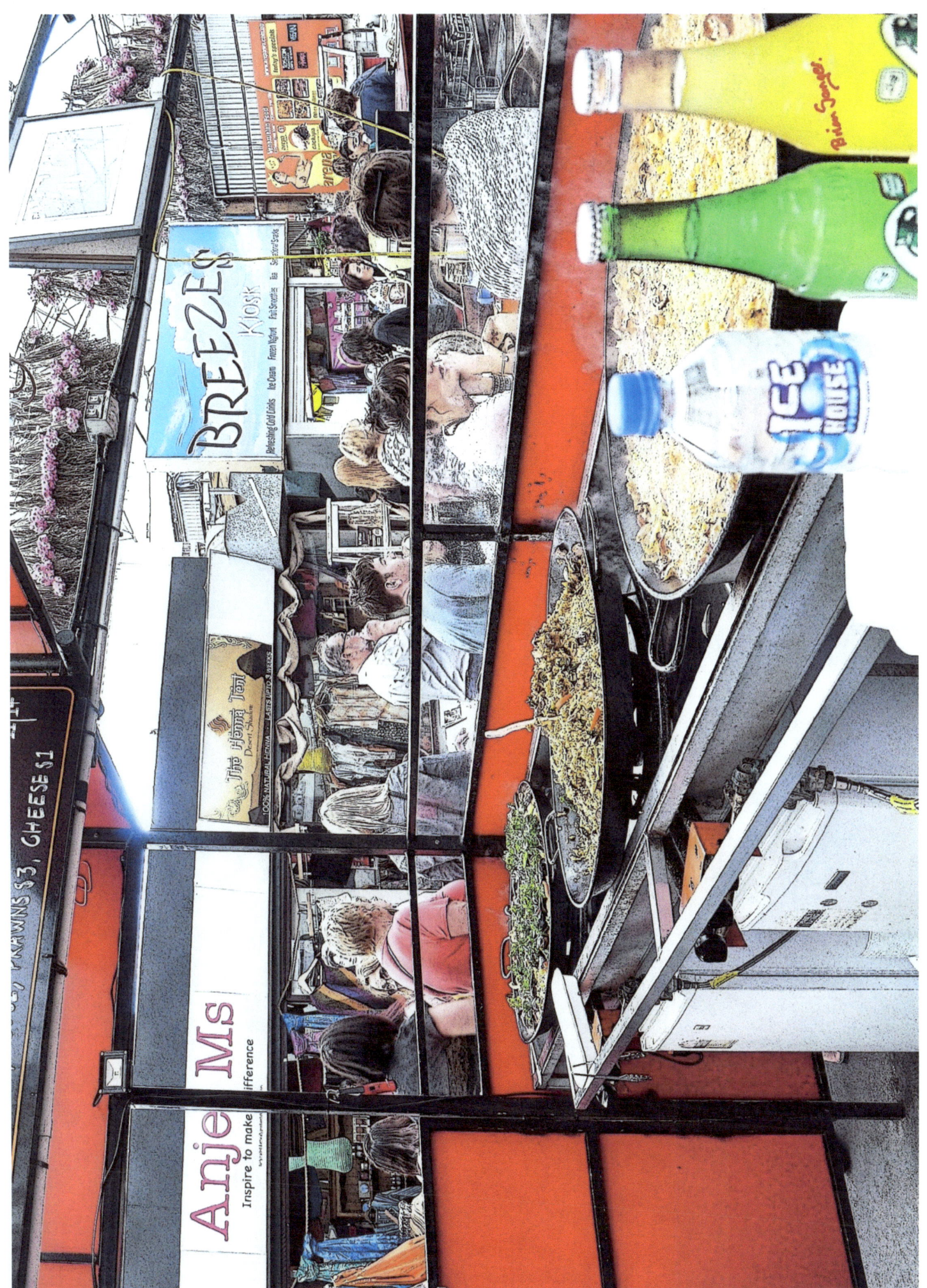

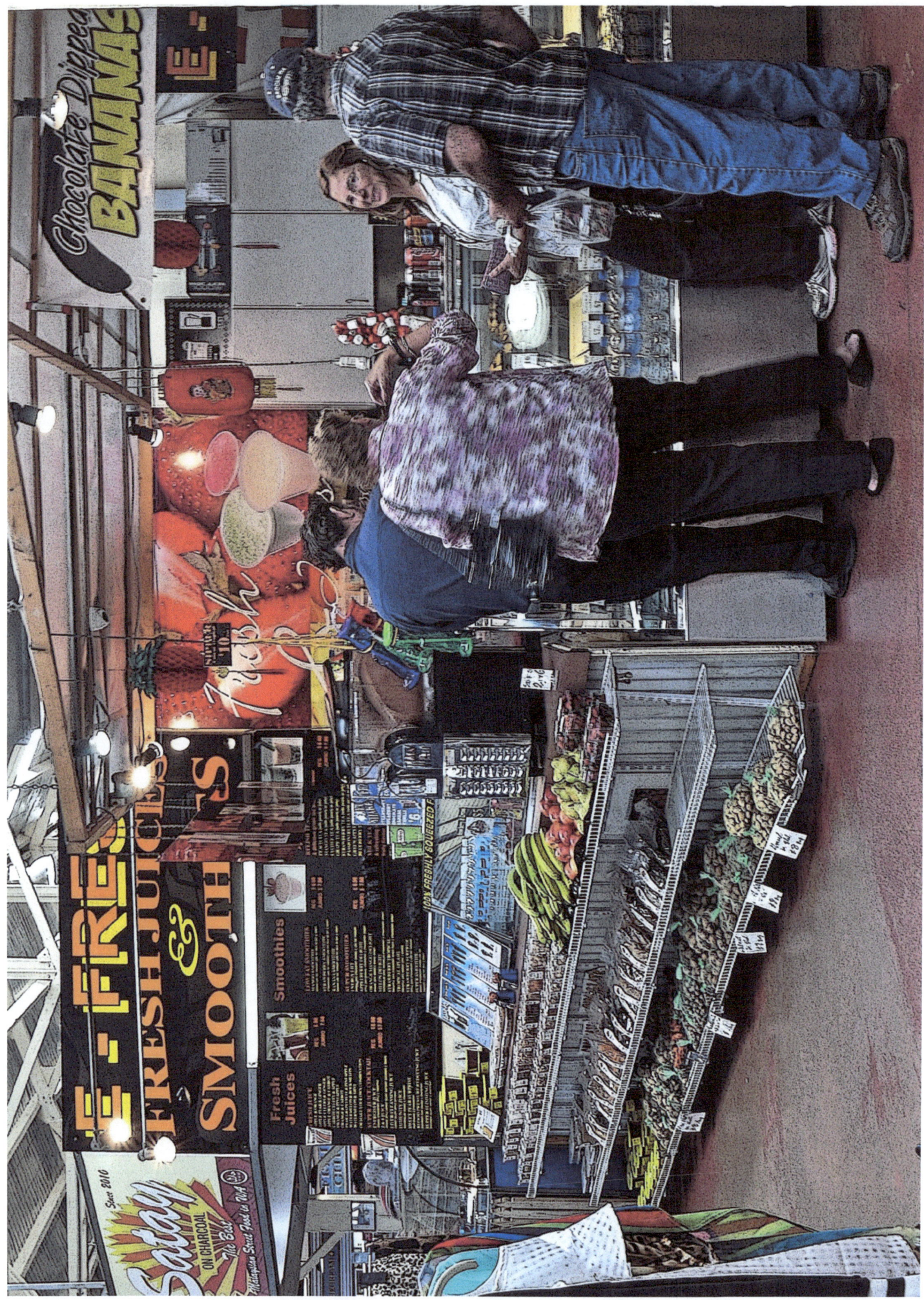

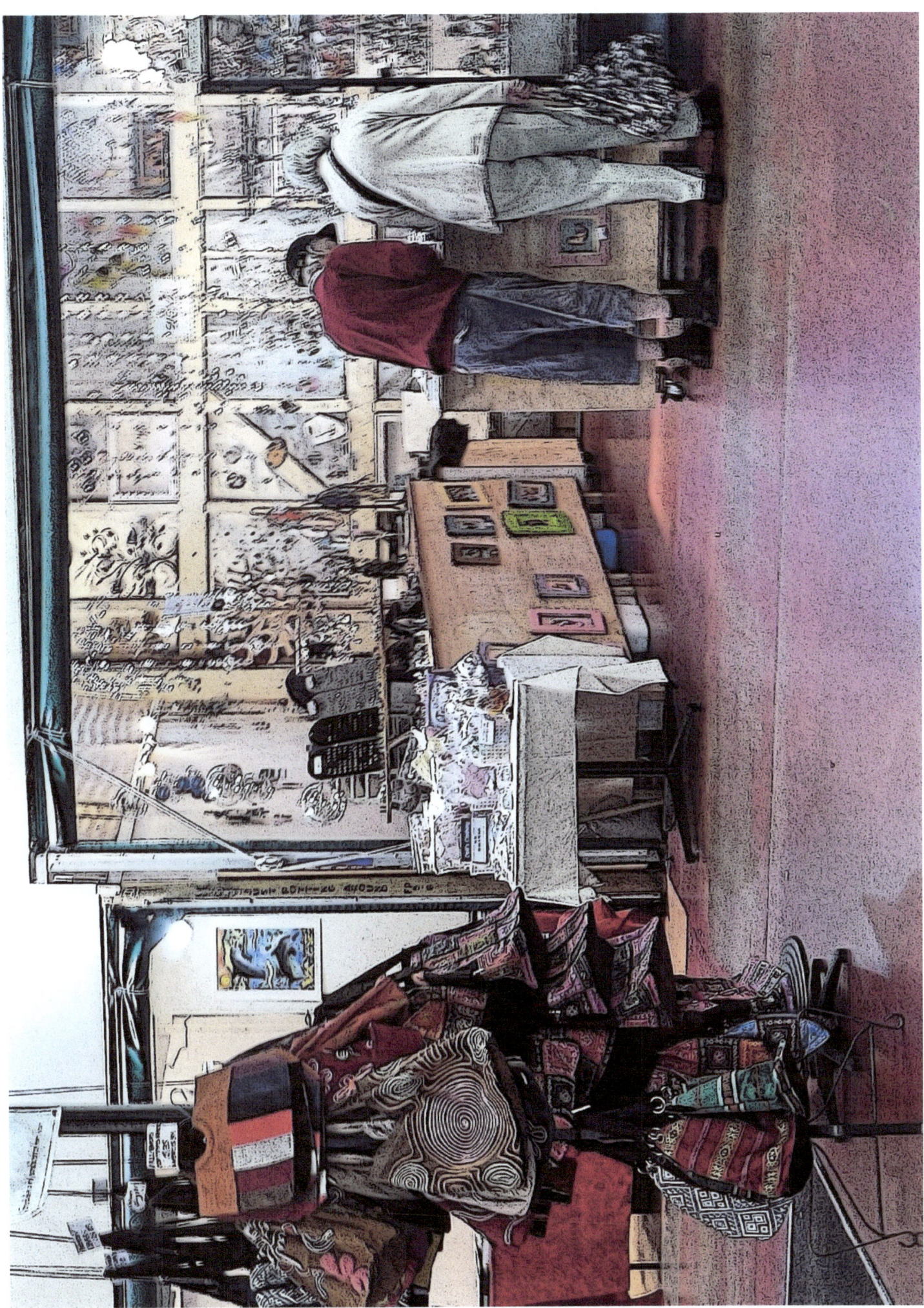

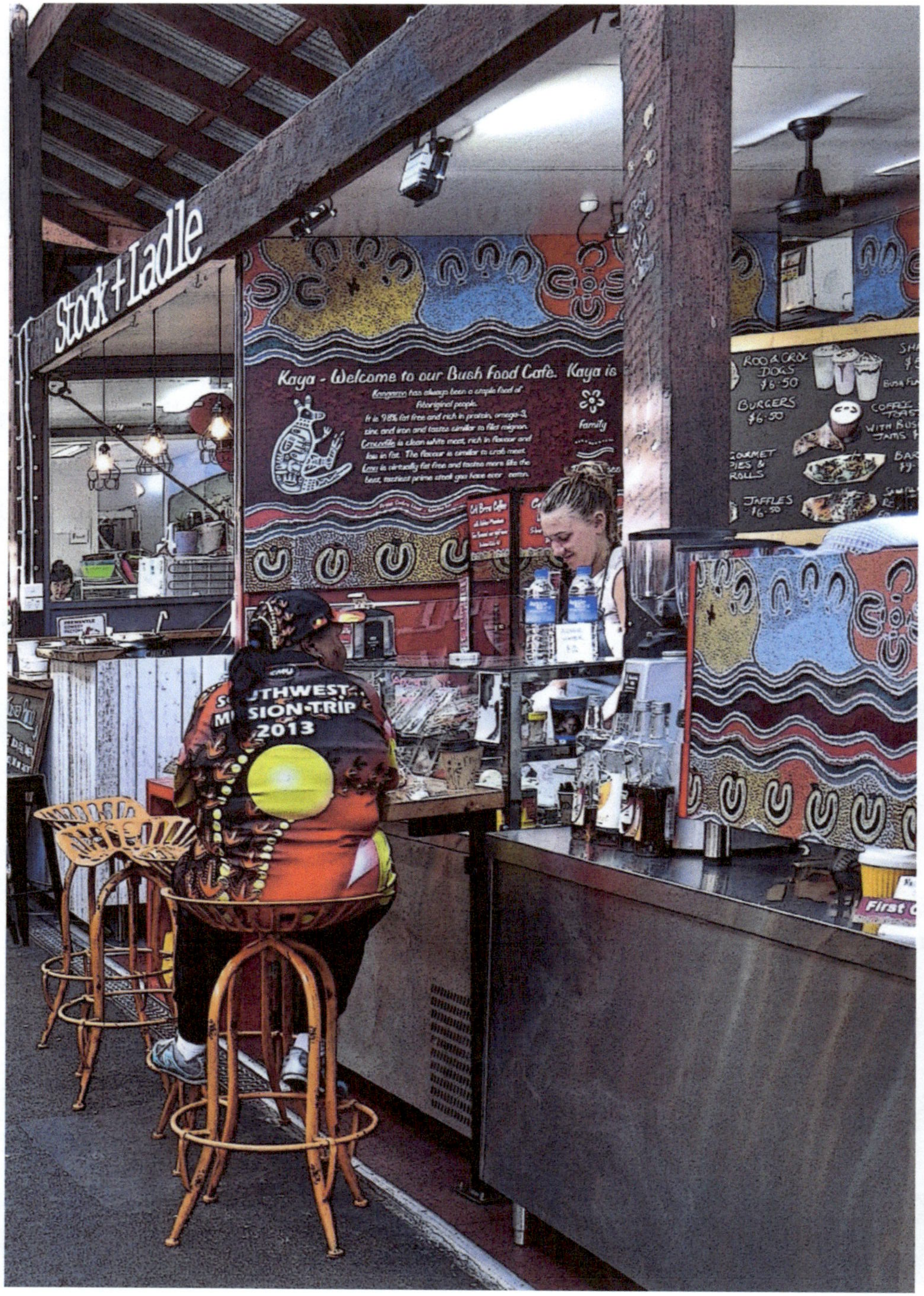
Stock + Ladle
Kaya - Welcome to our Bush Food Café. Kaya is
ROO & CROC DOGS $6.50
BURGERS $6.50
GOURMET PIES & ROLLS
JAFFLES $6.50
SOUTHWEST MISSION TRIP 2013
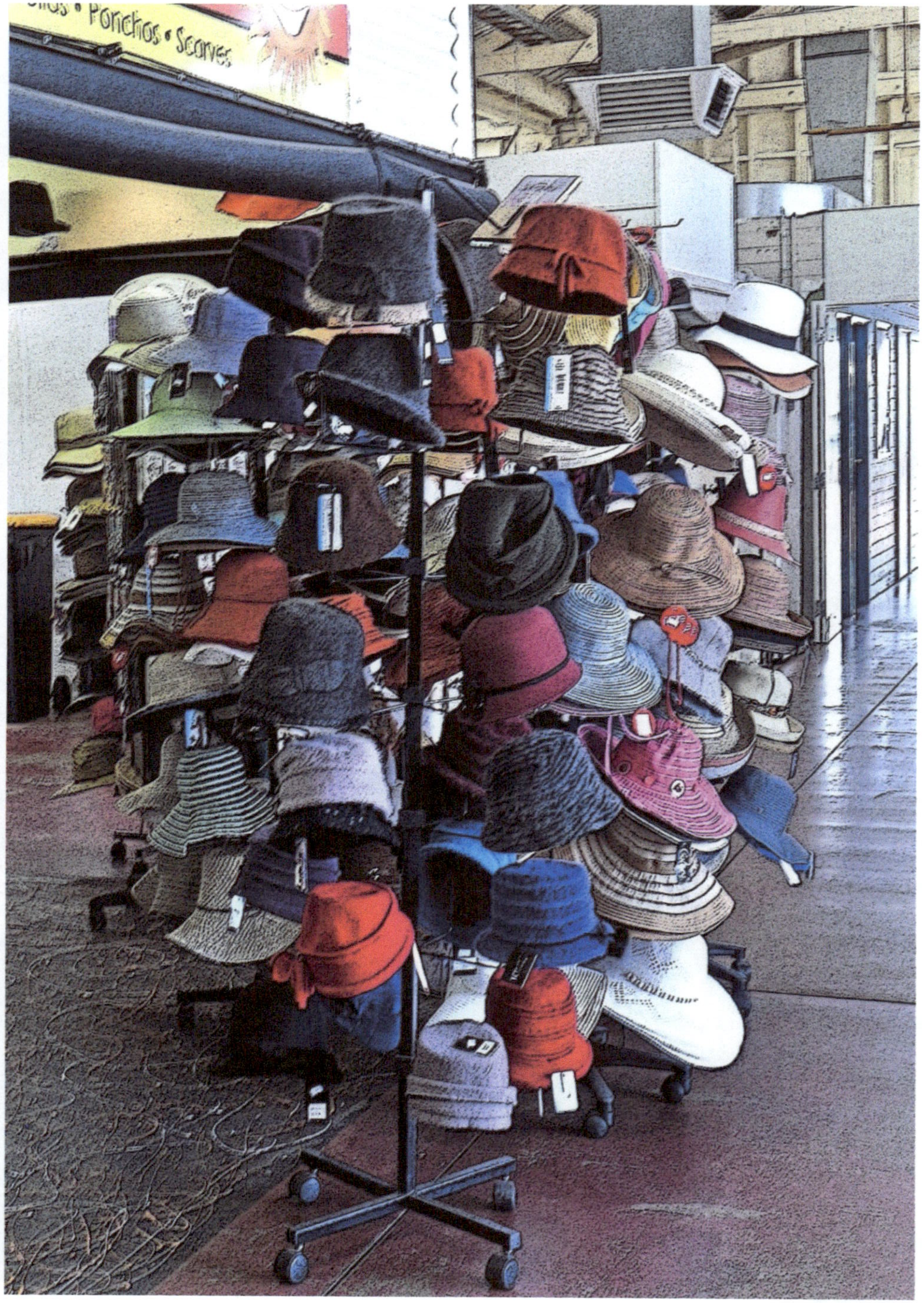
Ponchos • Scarves

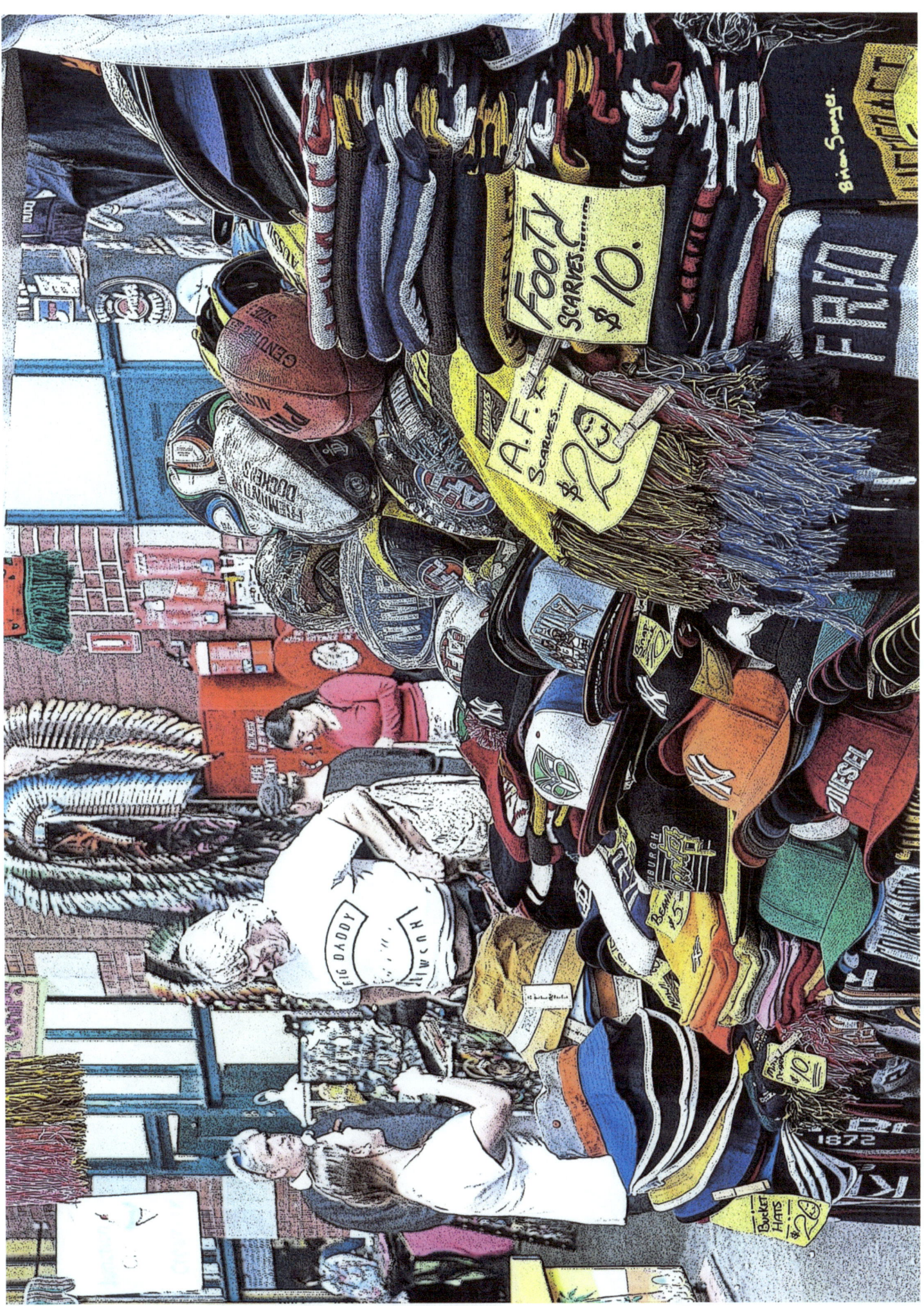

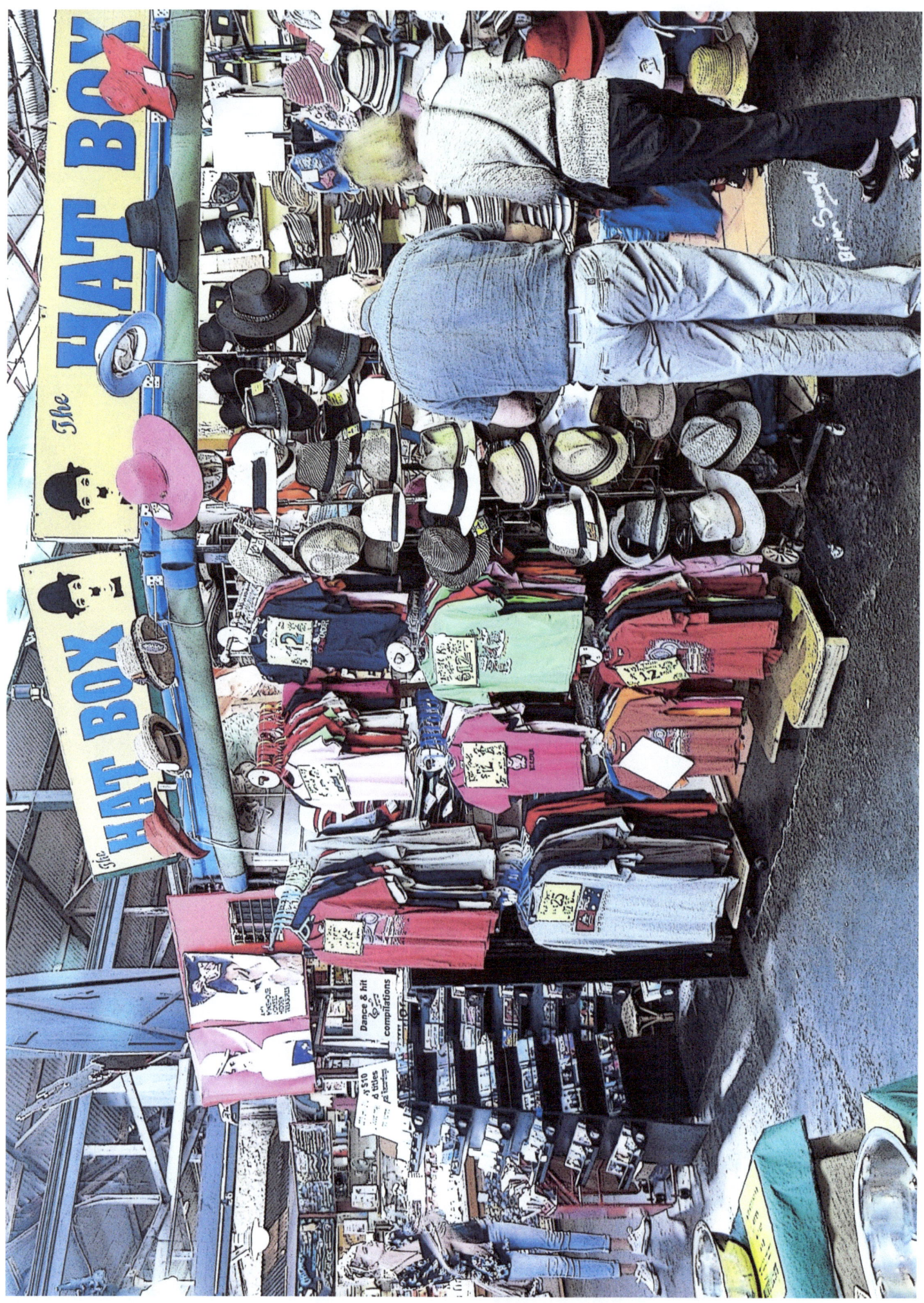

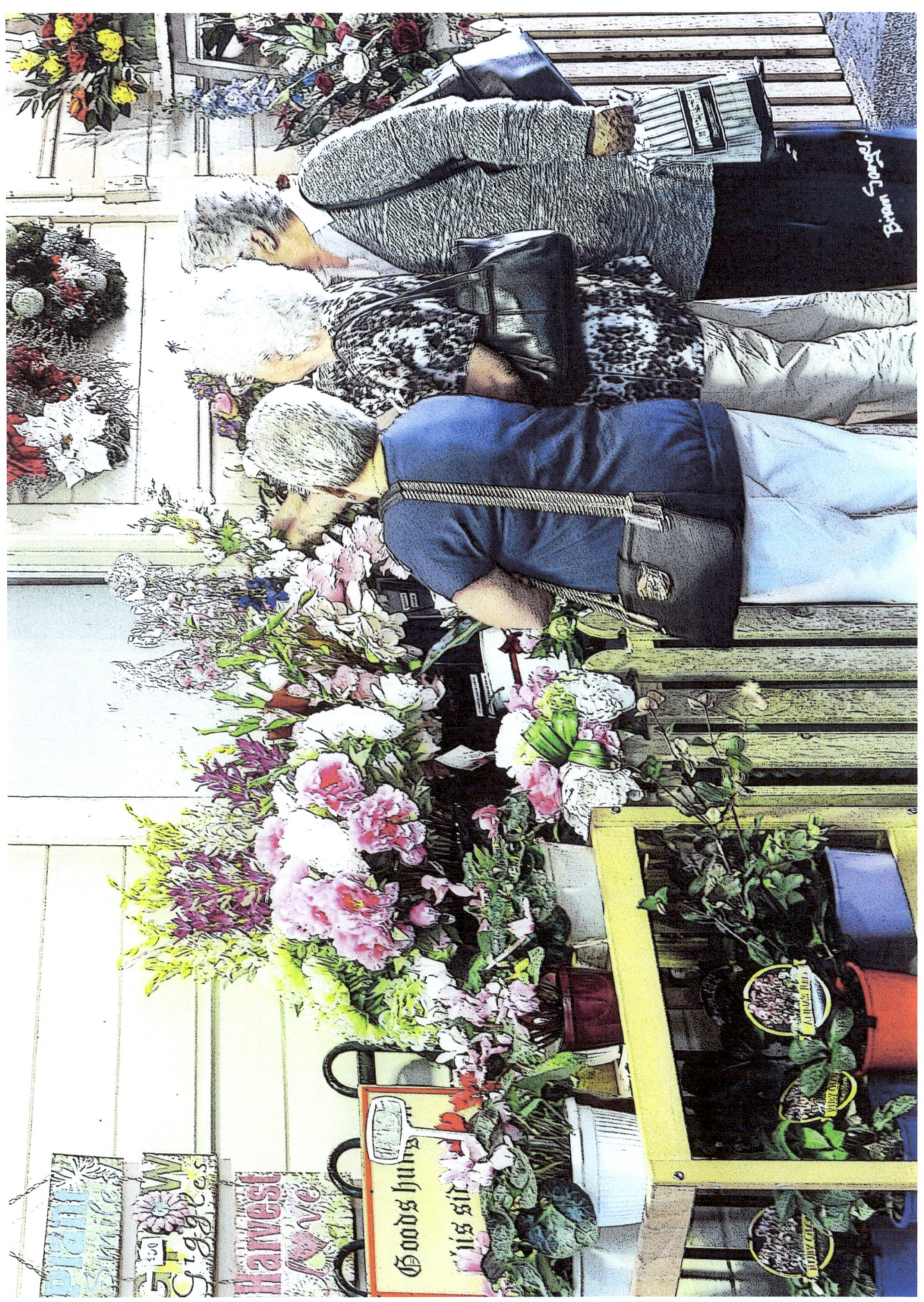

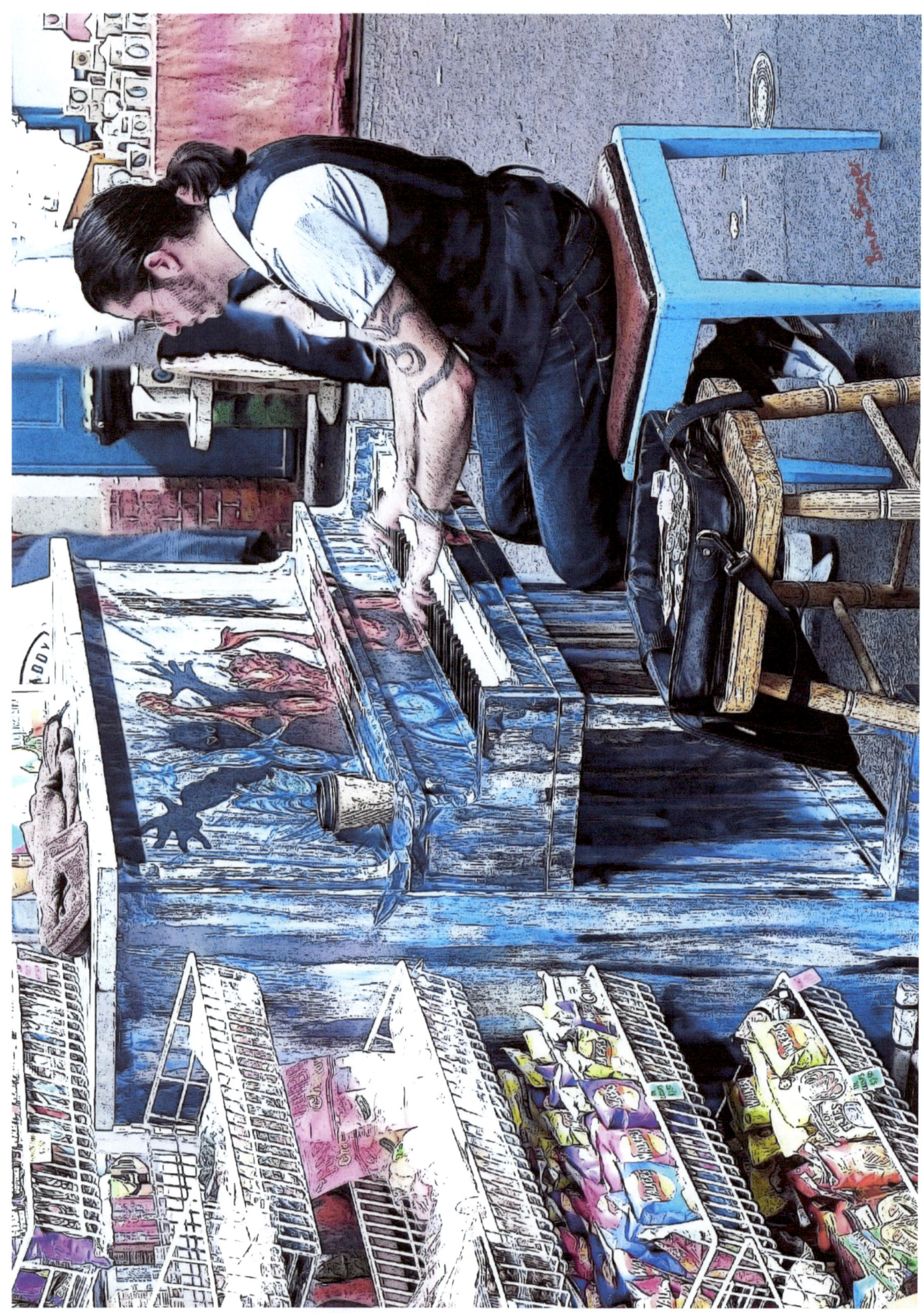

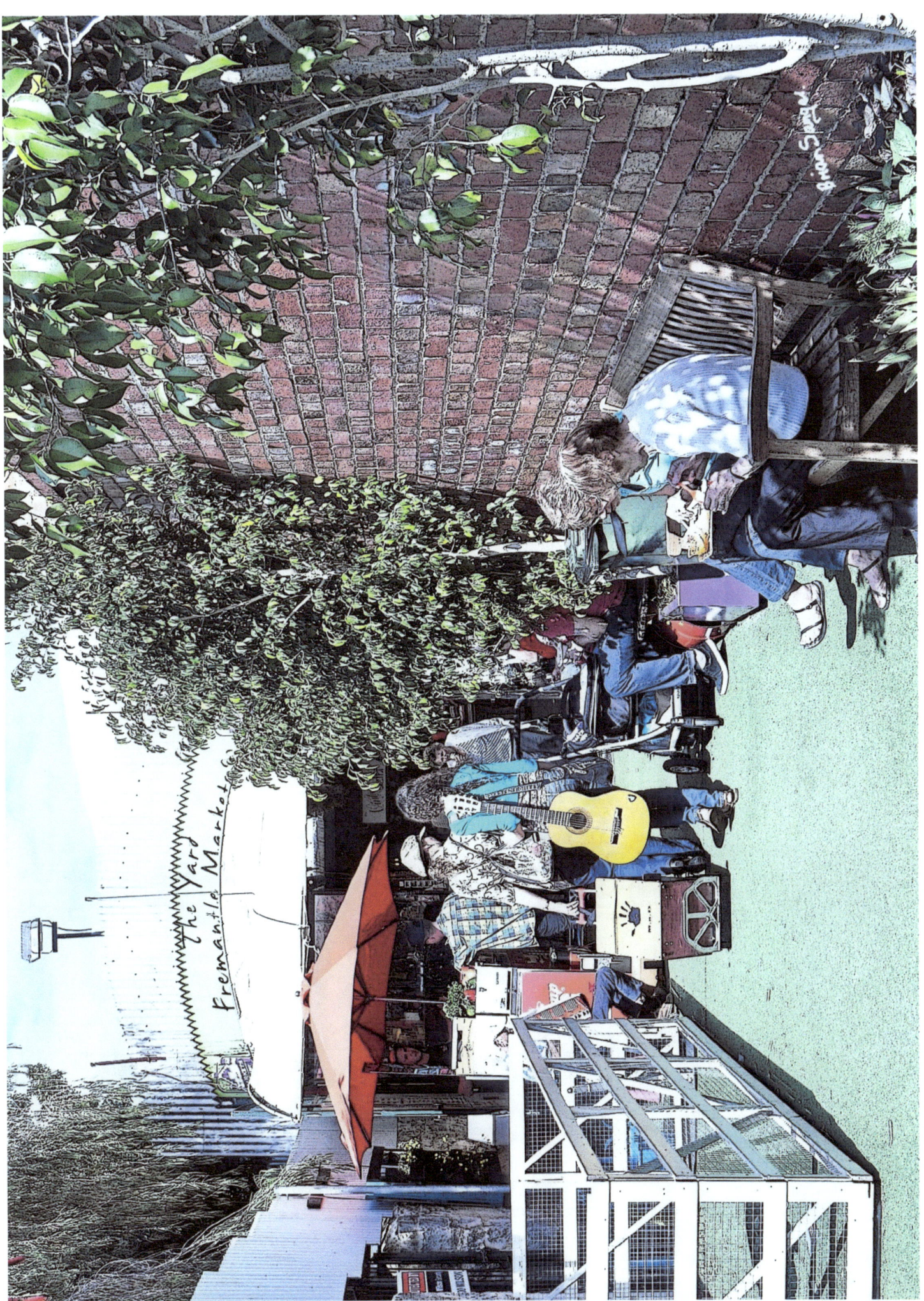

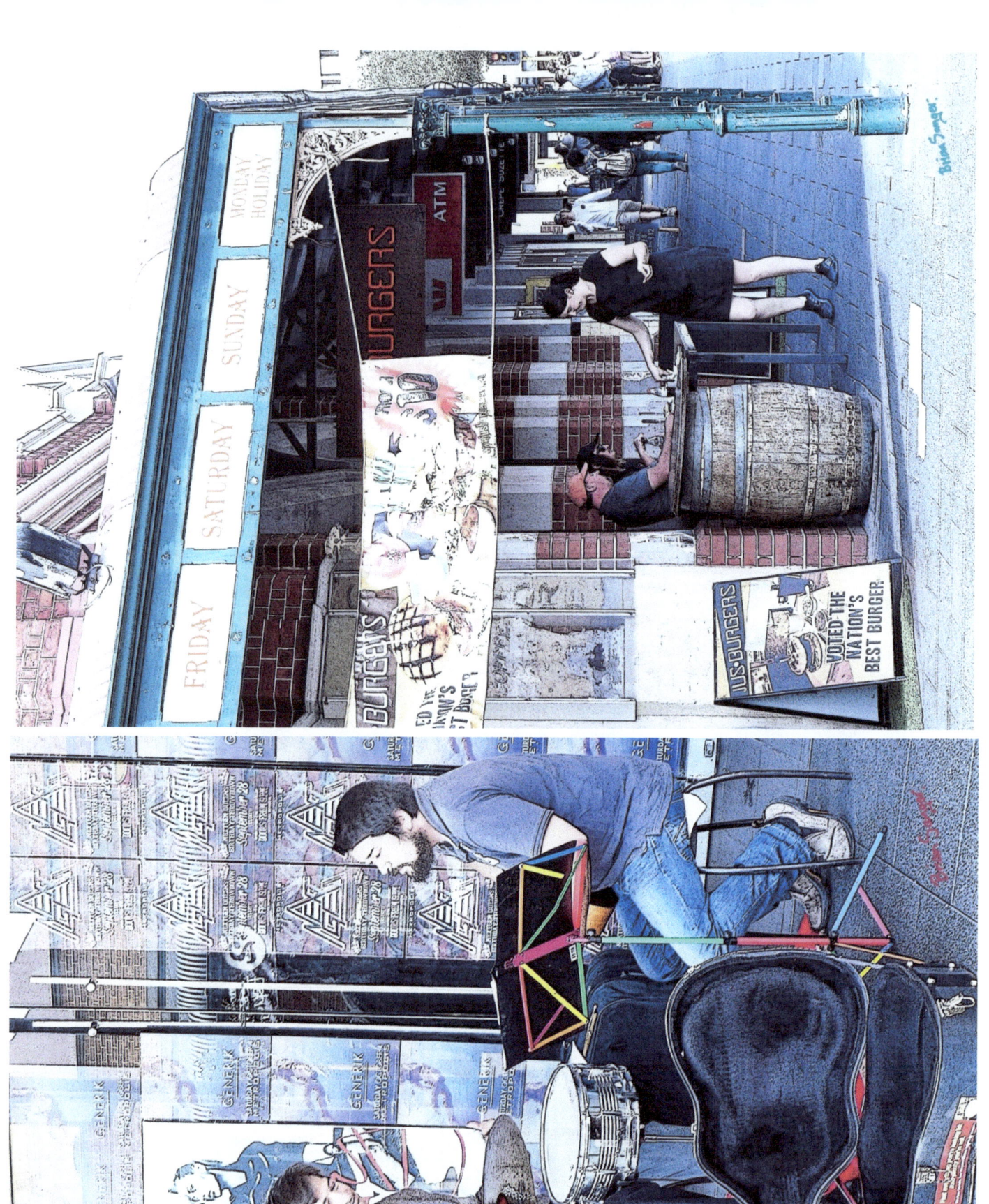

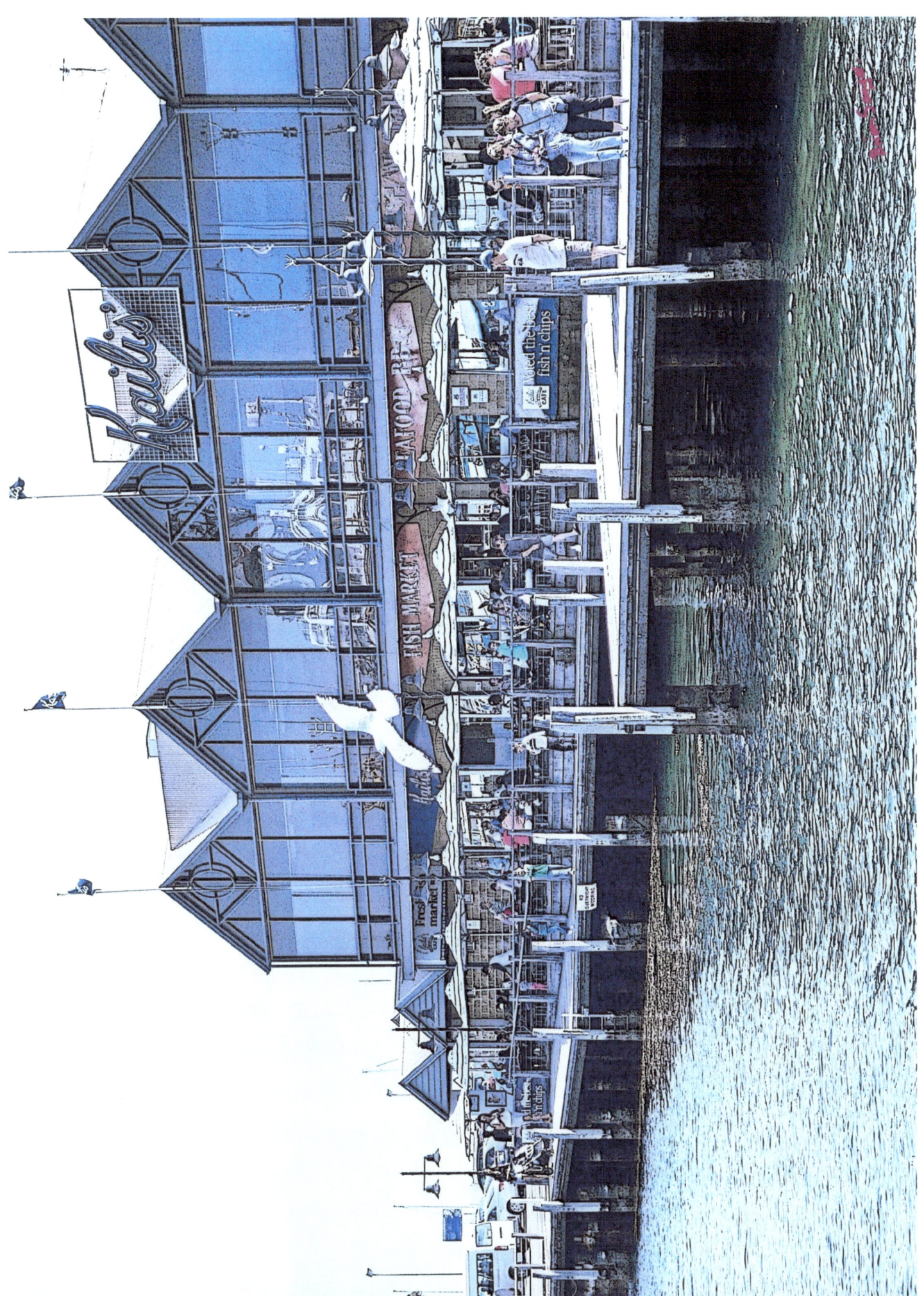

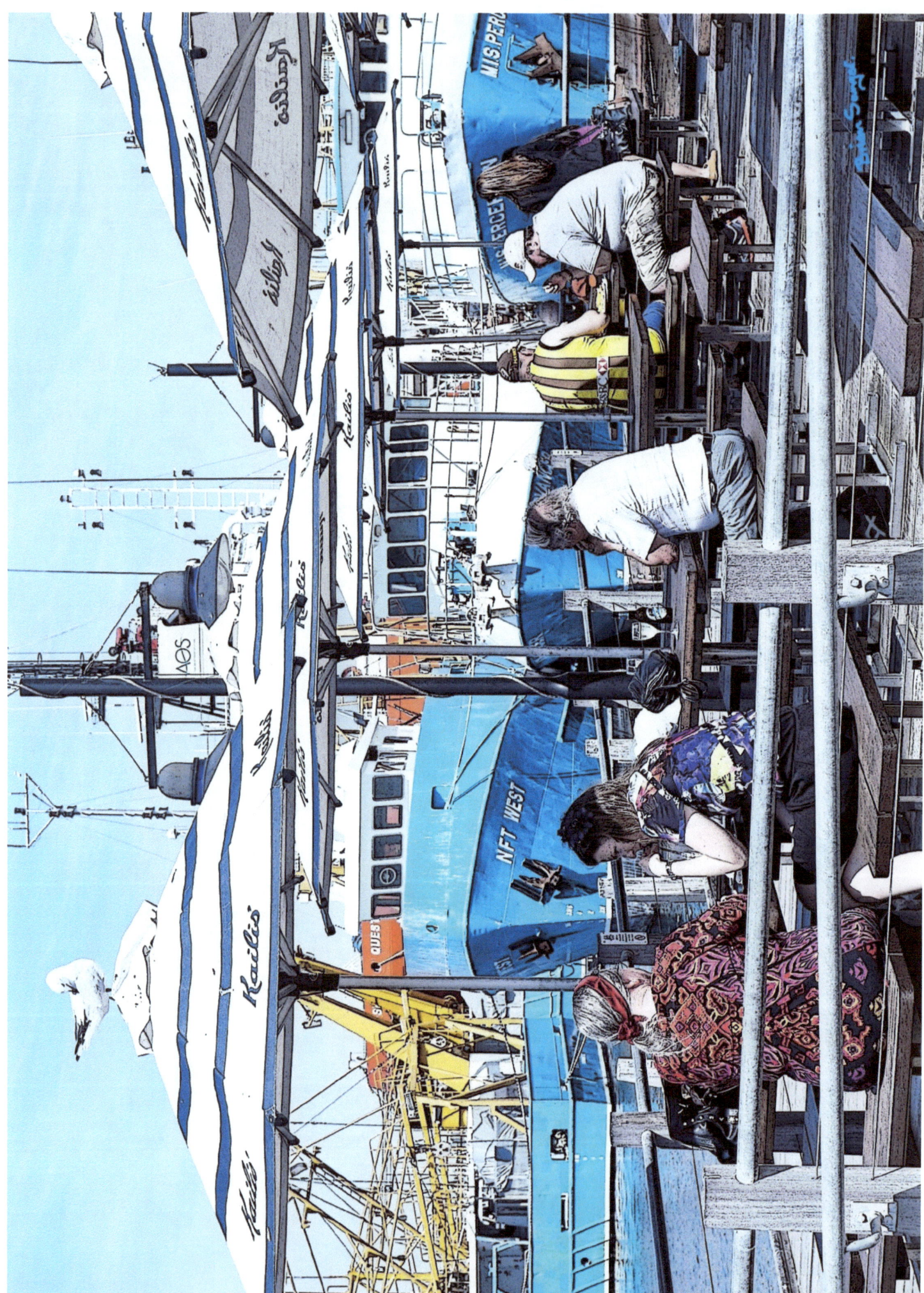

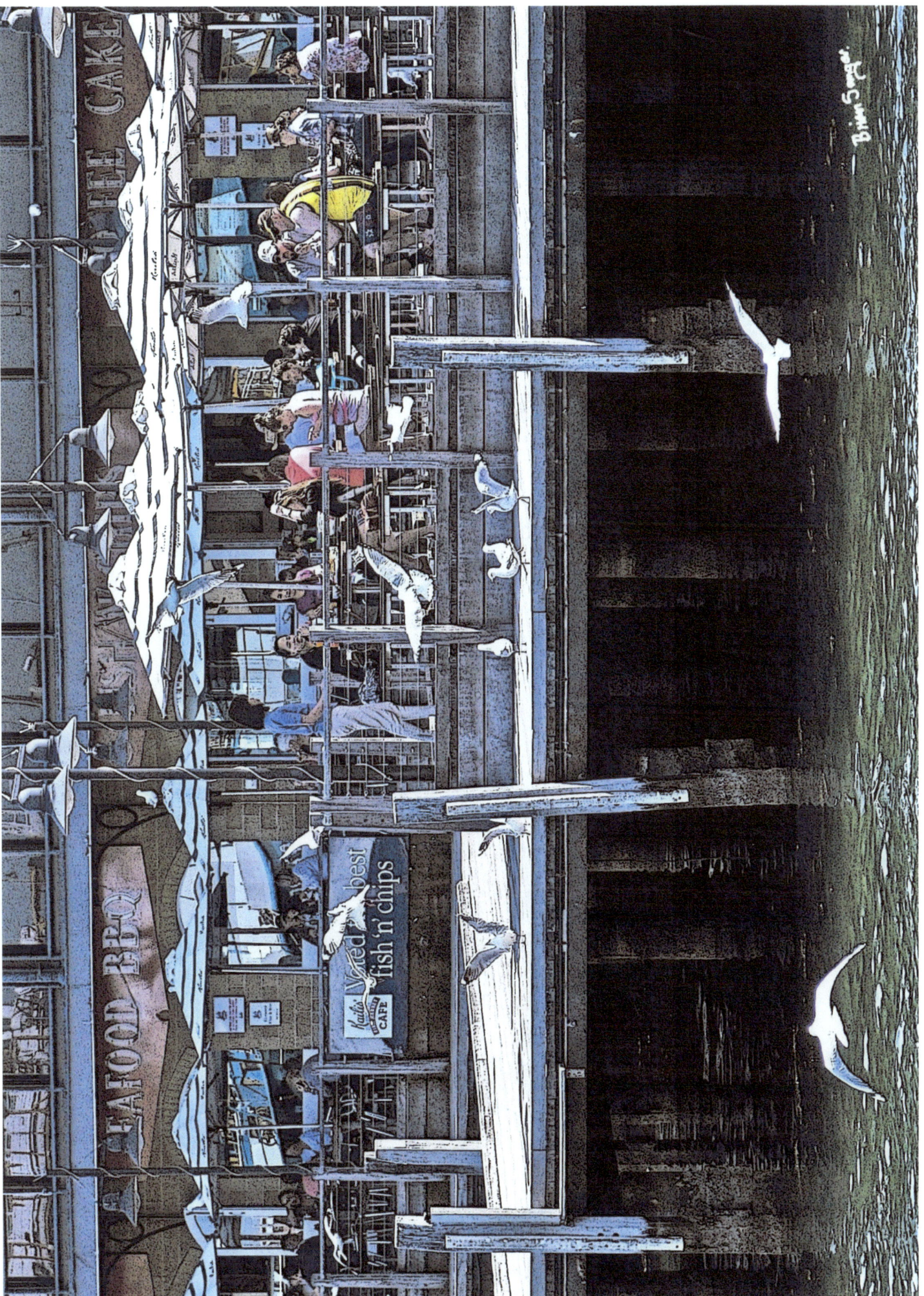

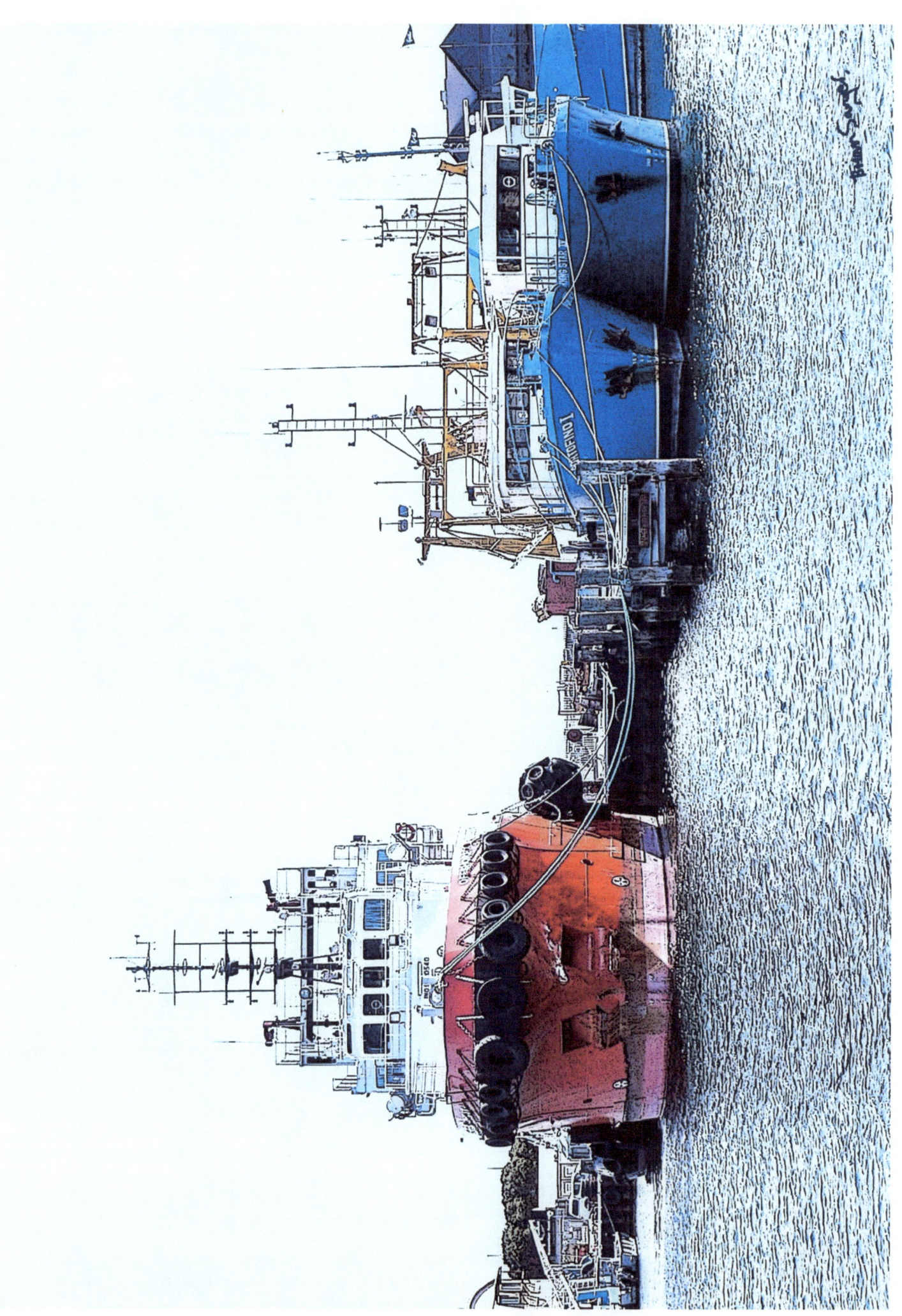

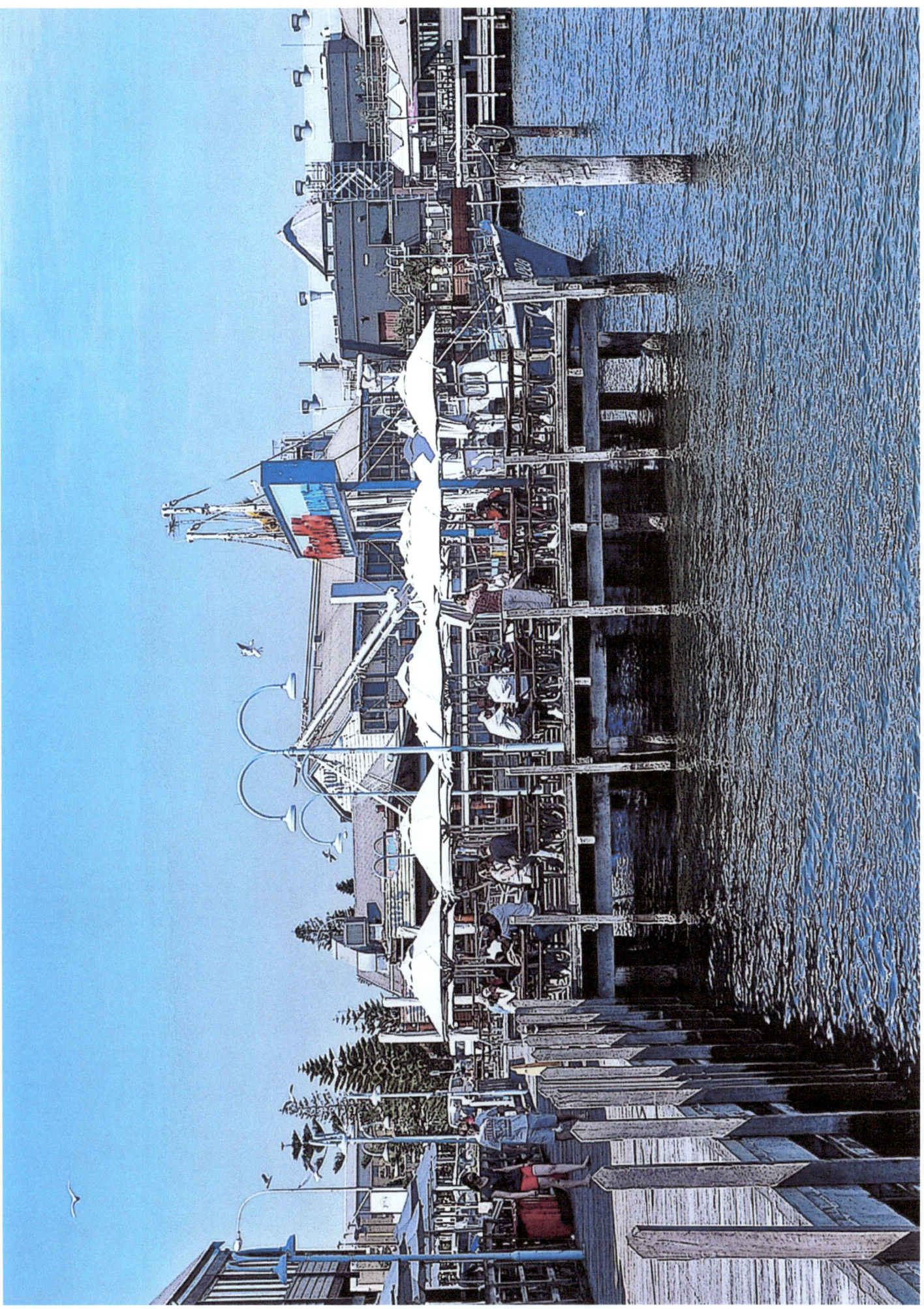

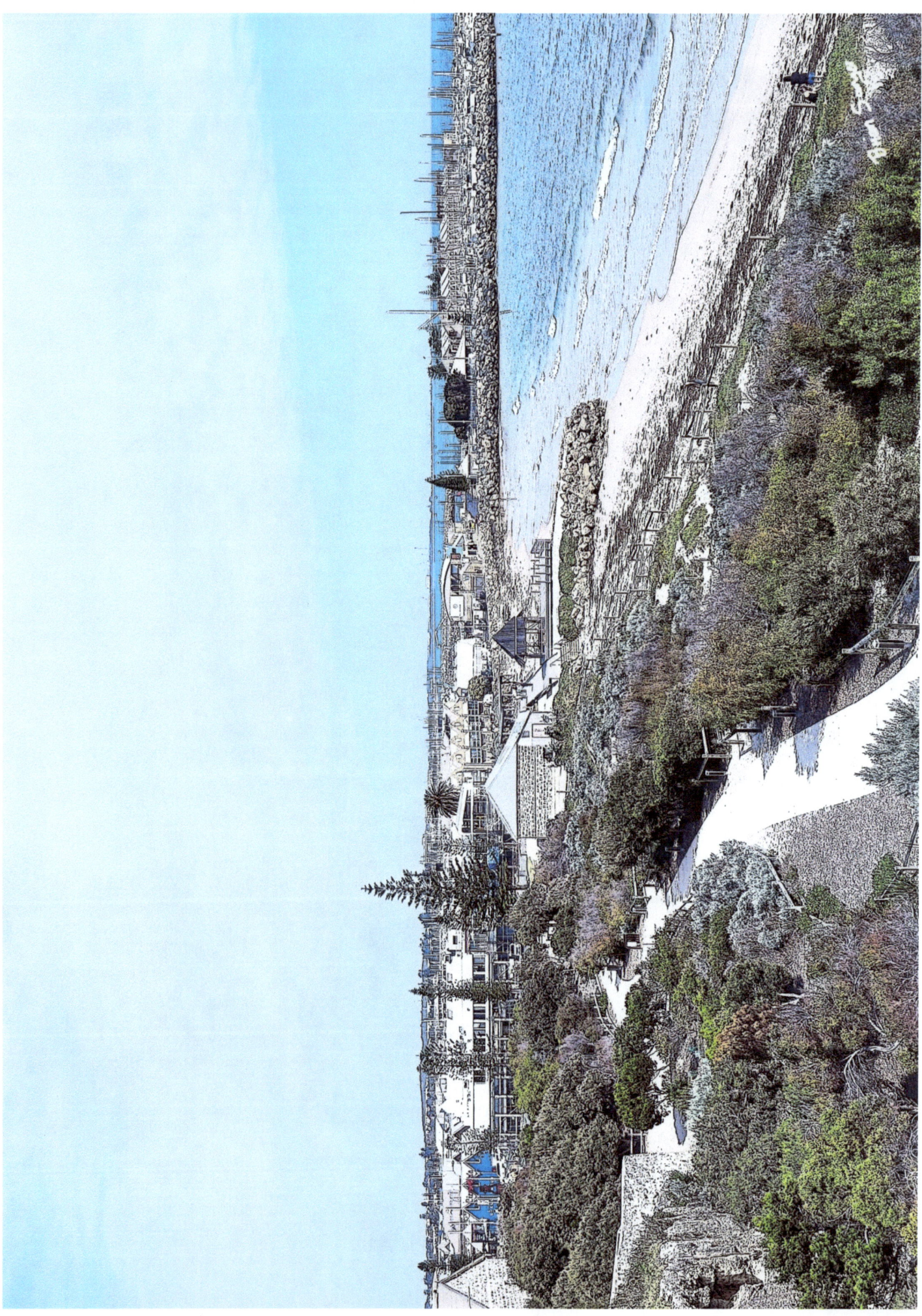

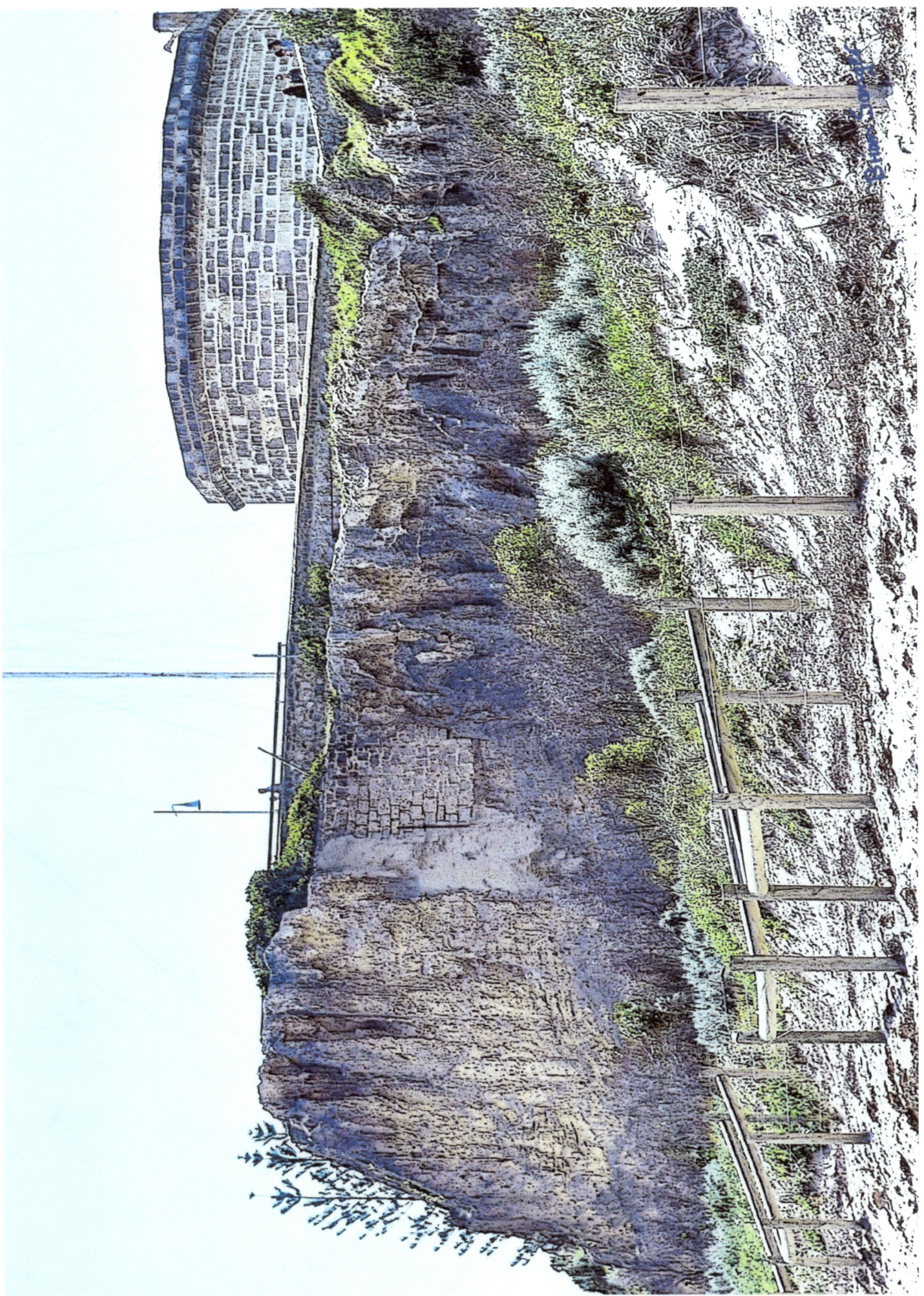

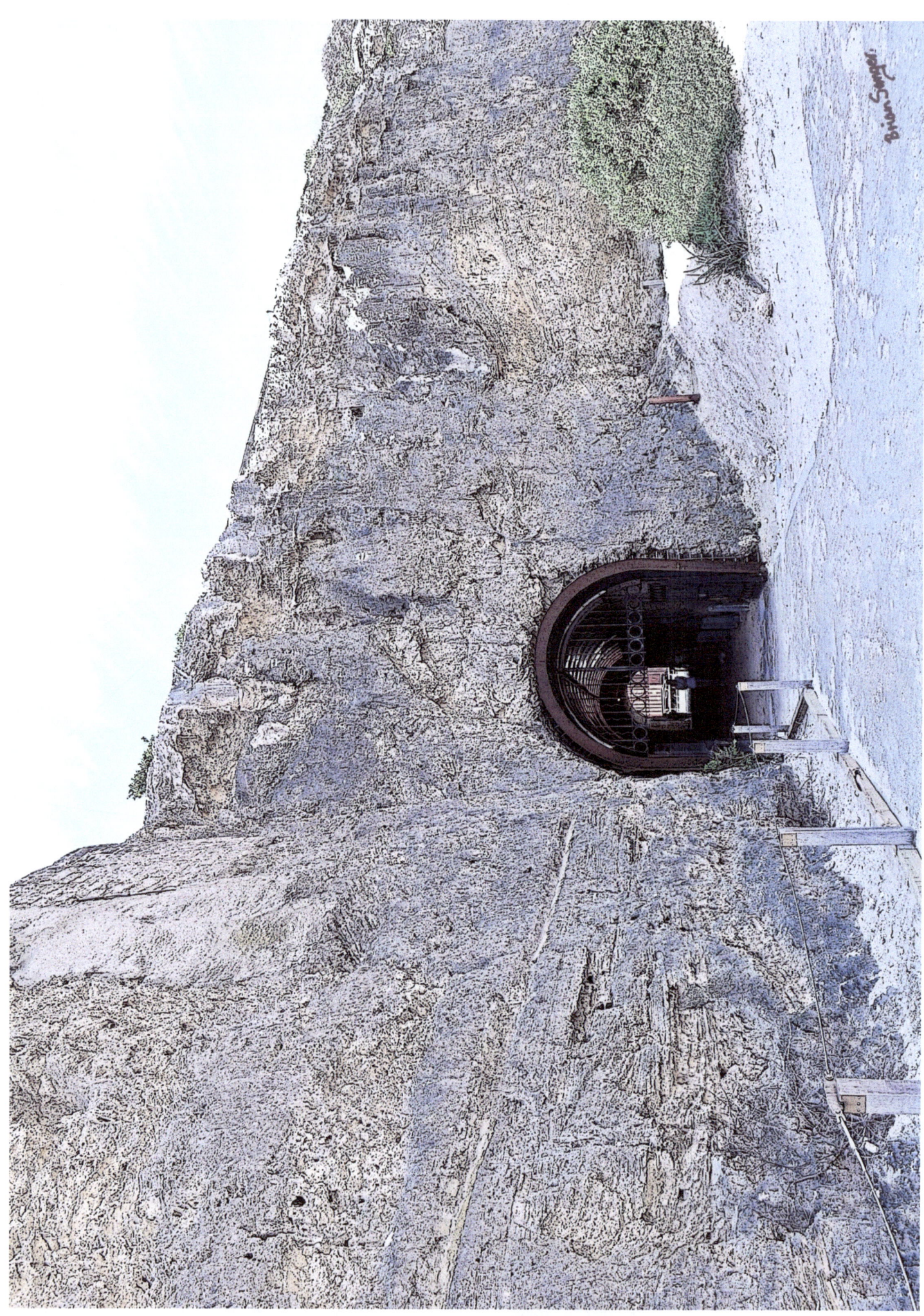

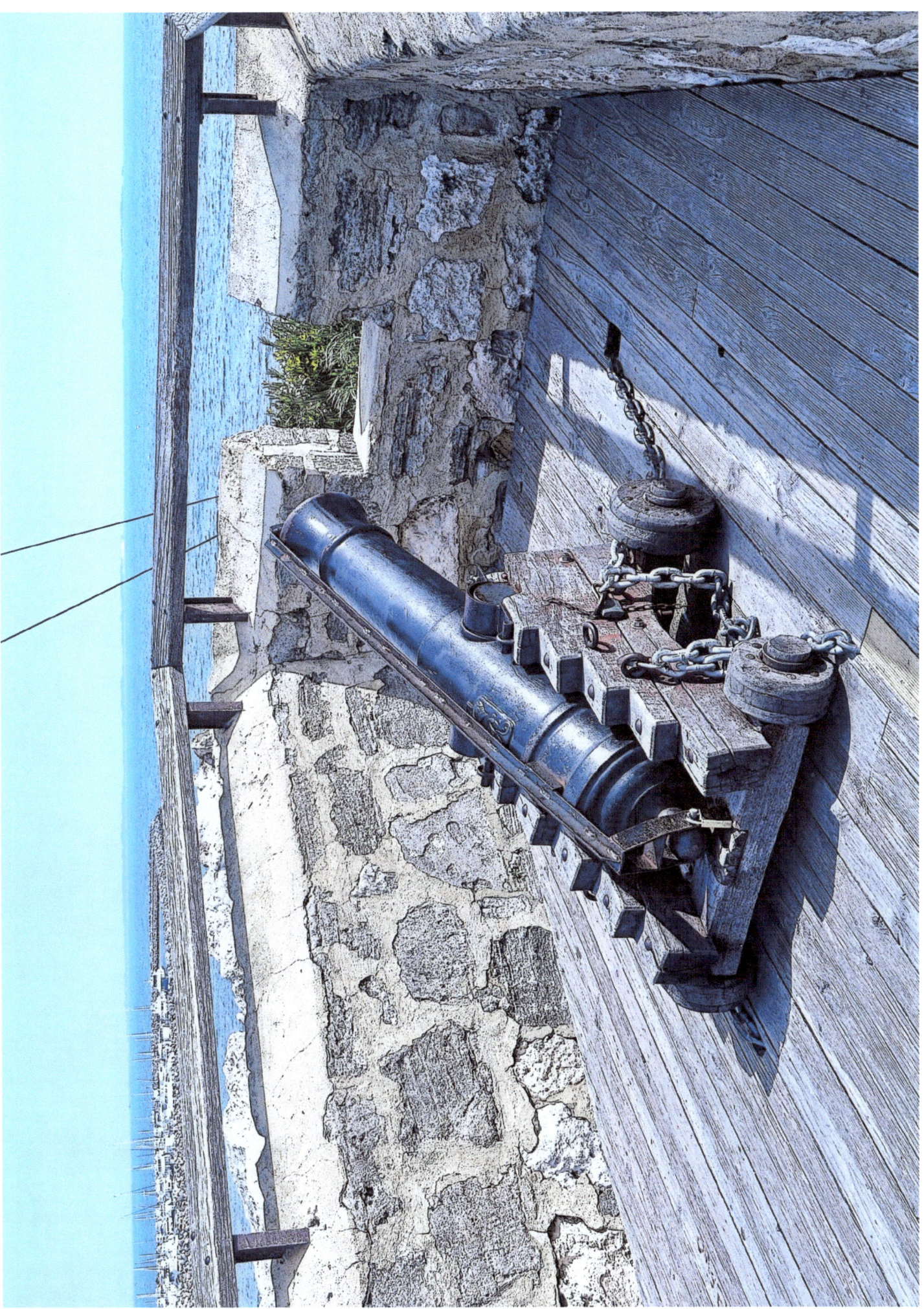

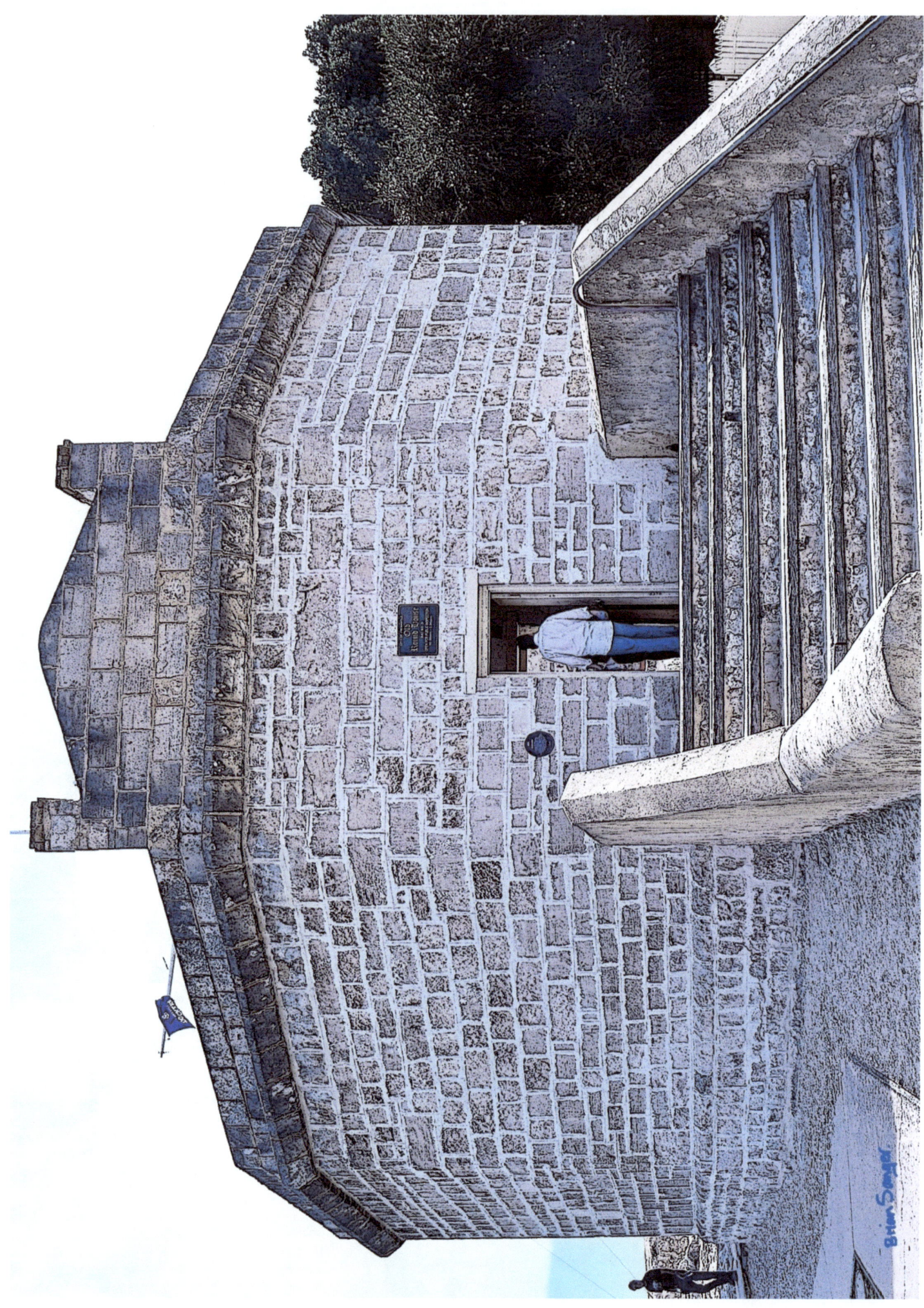

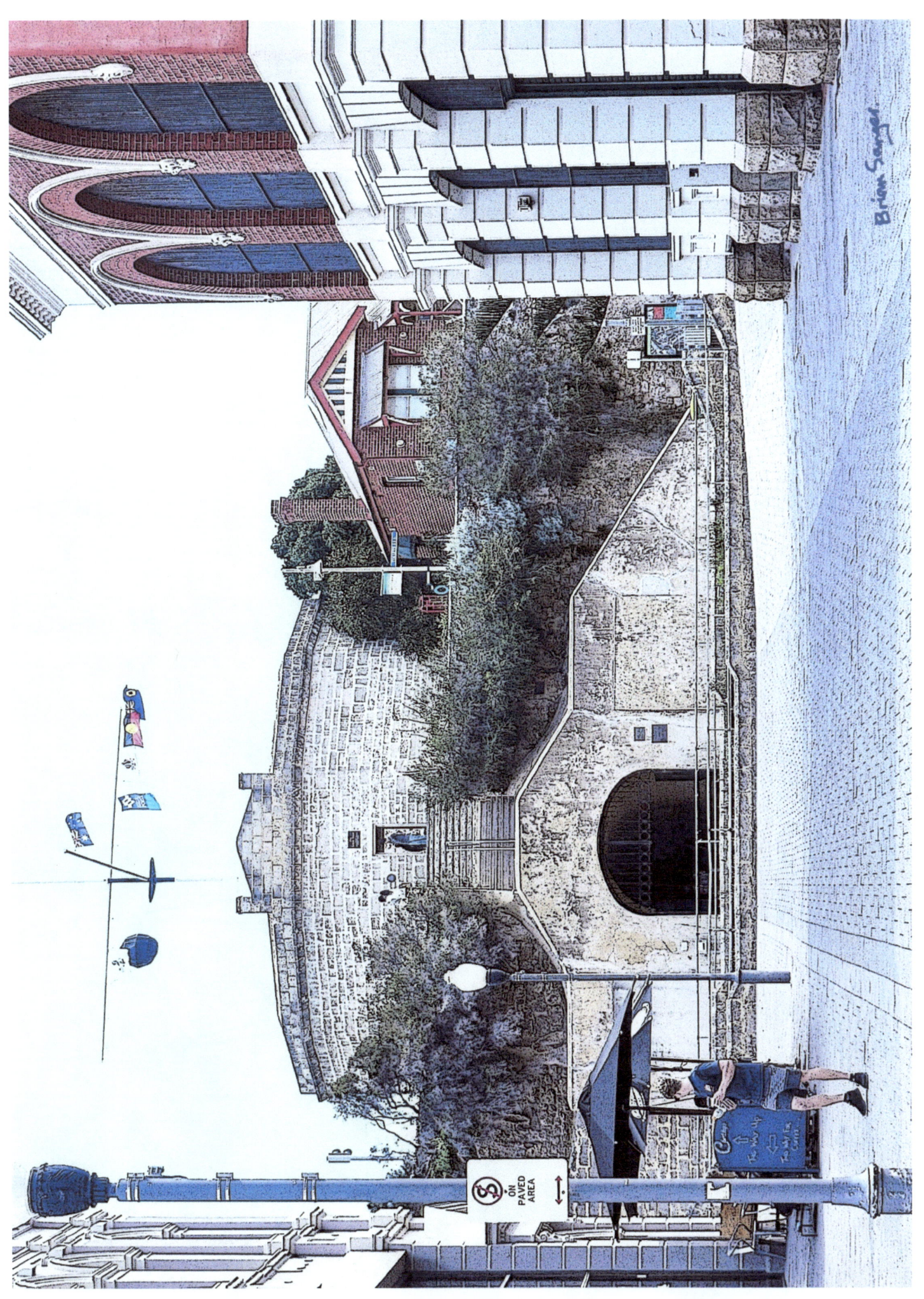

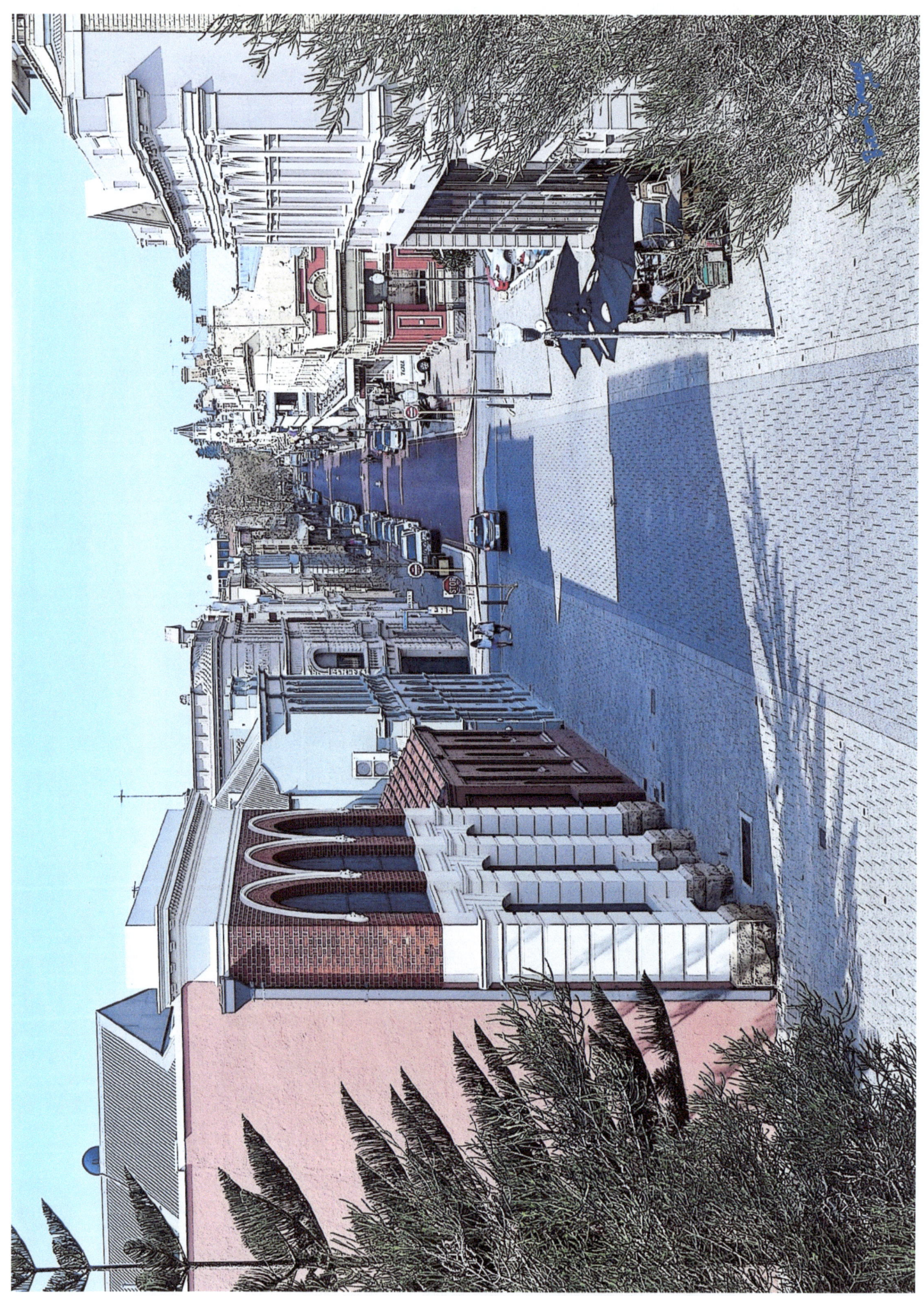

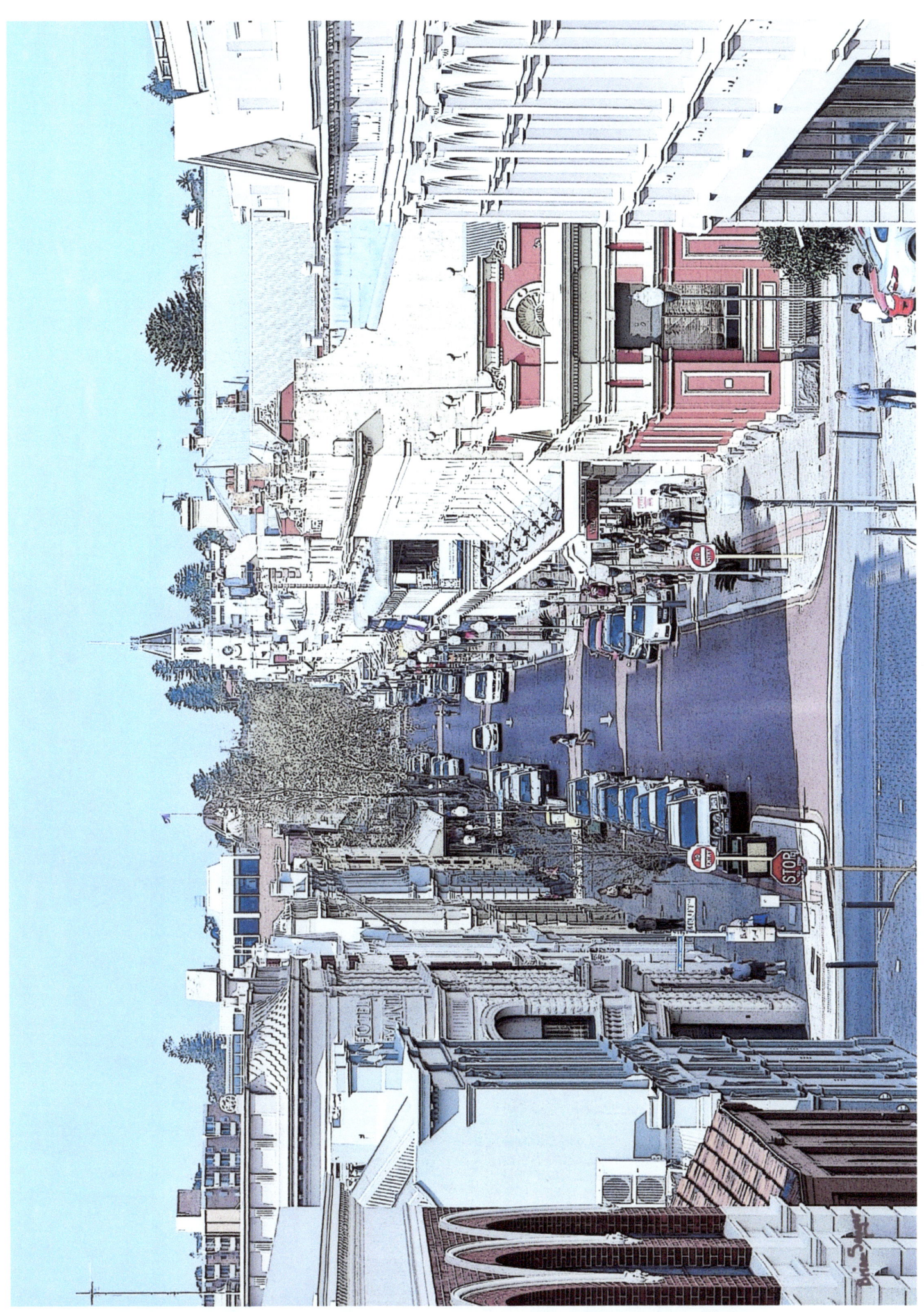

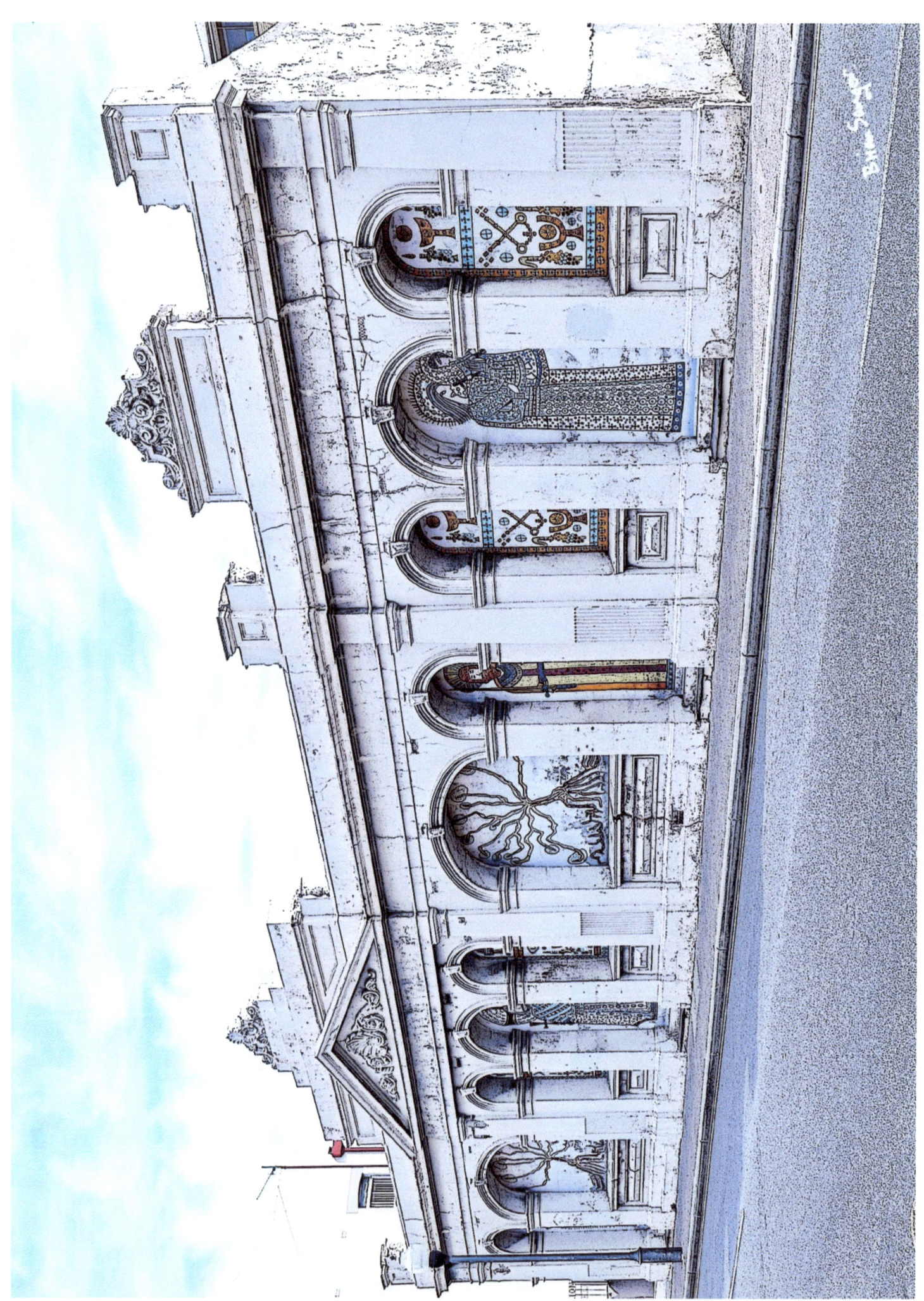

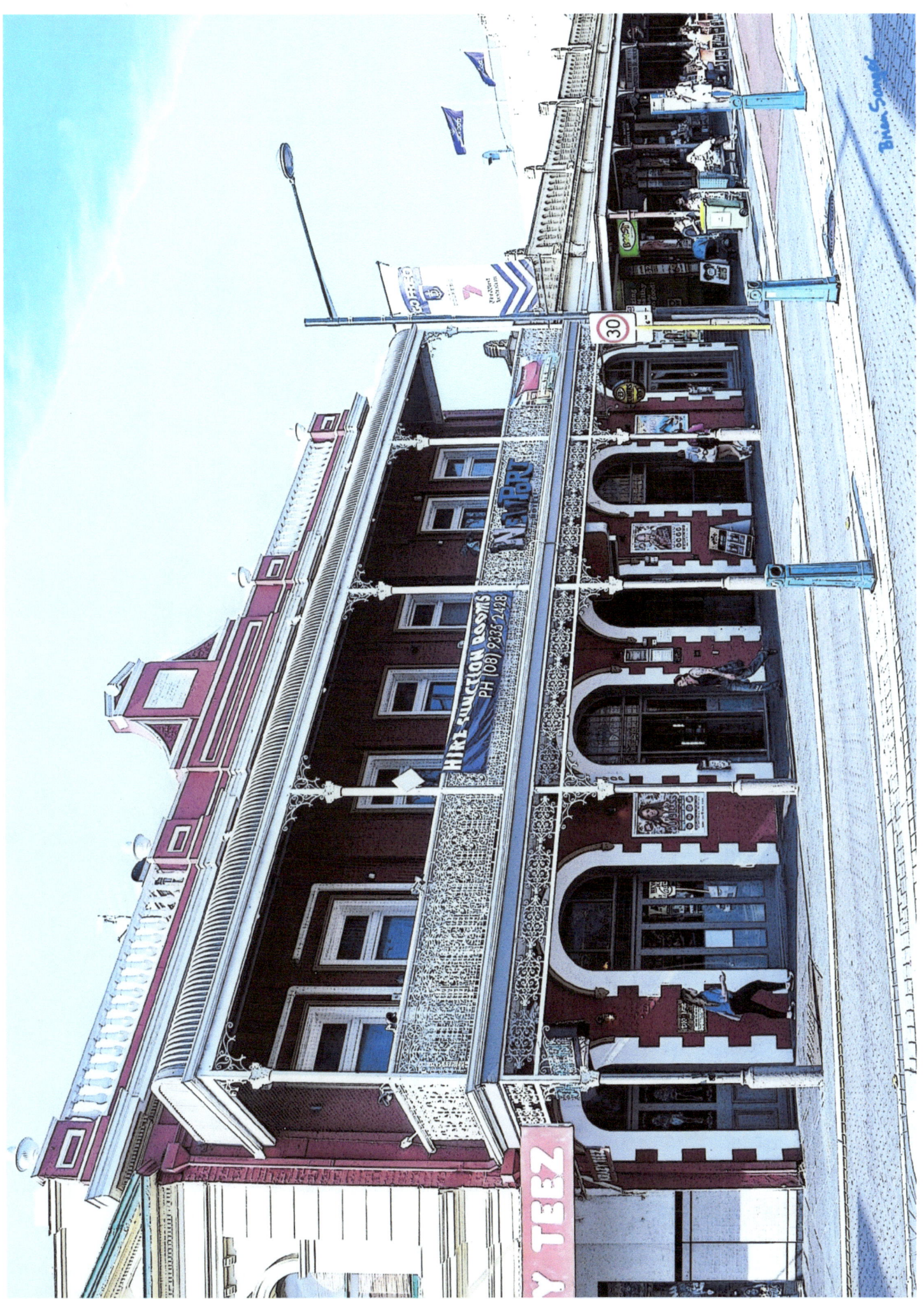

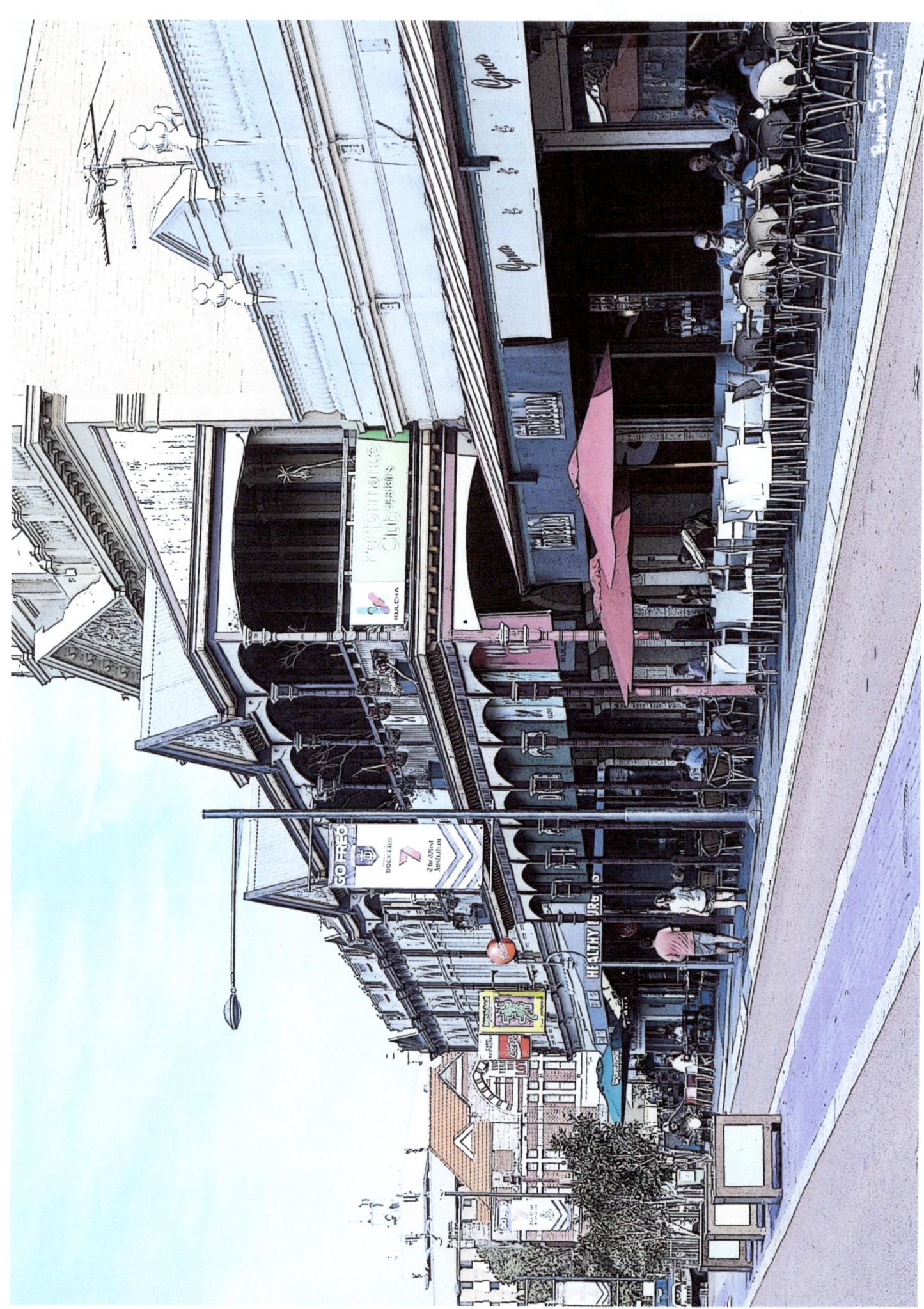

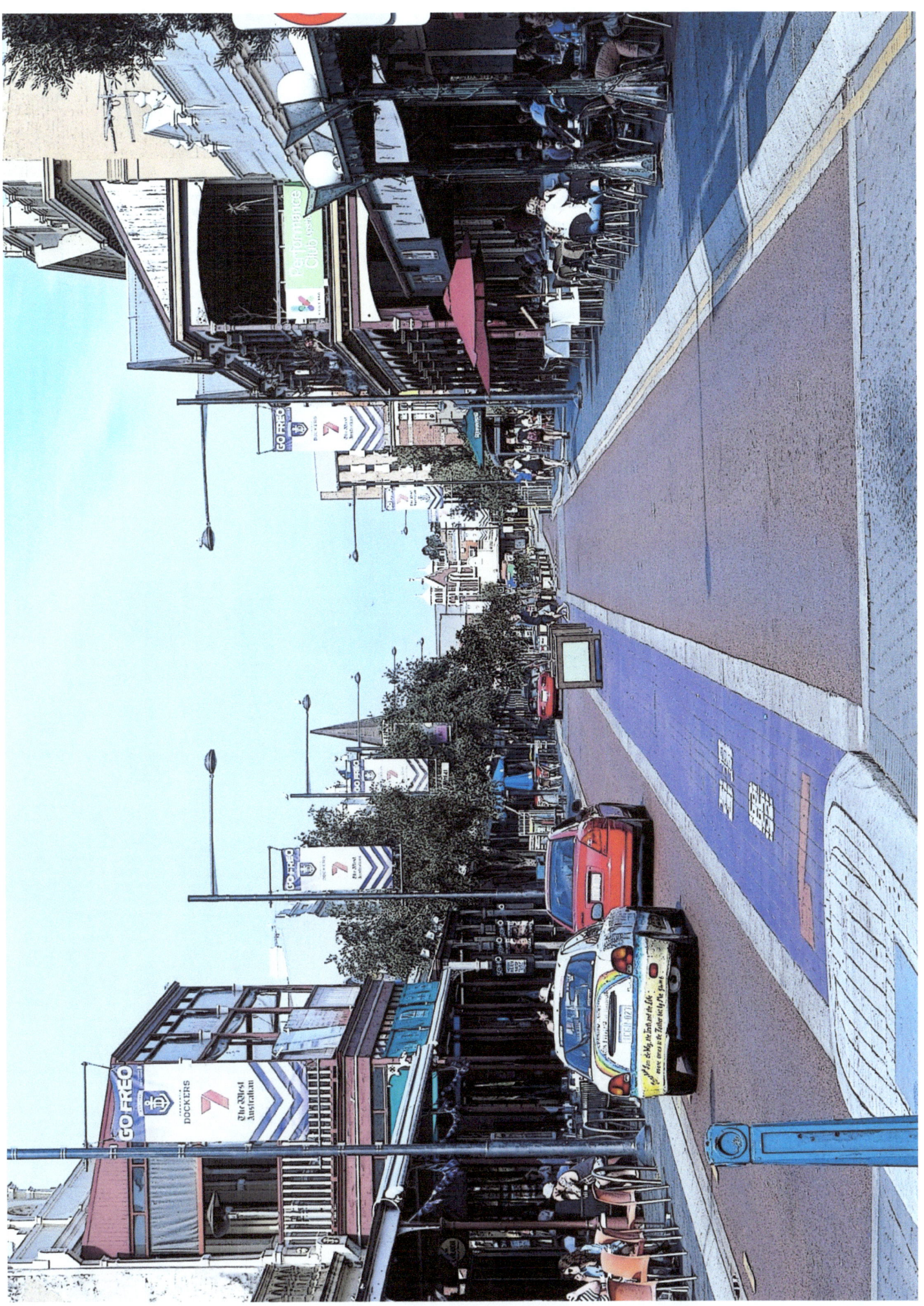

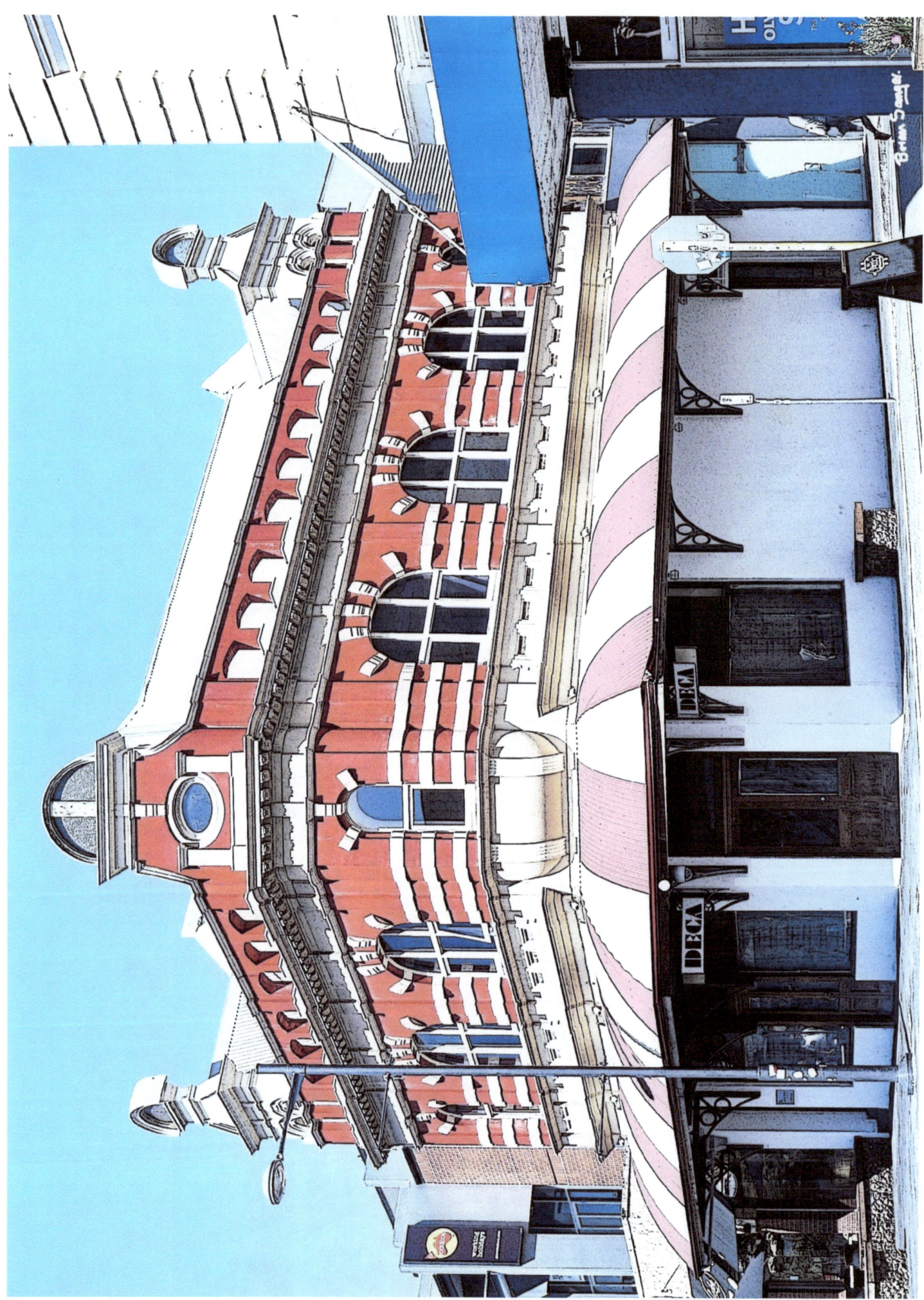

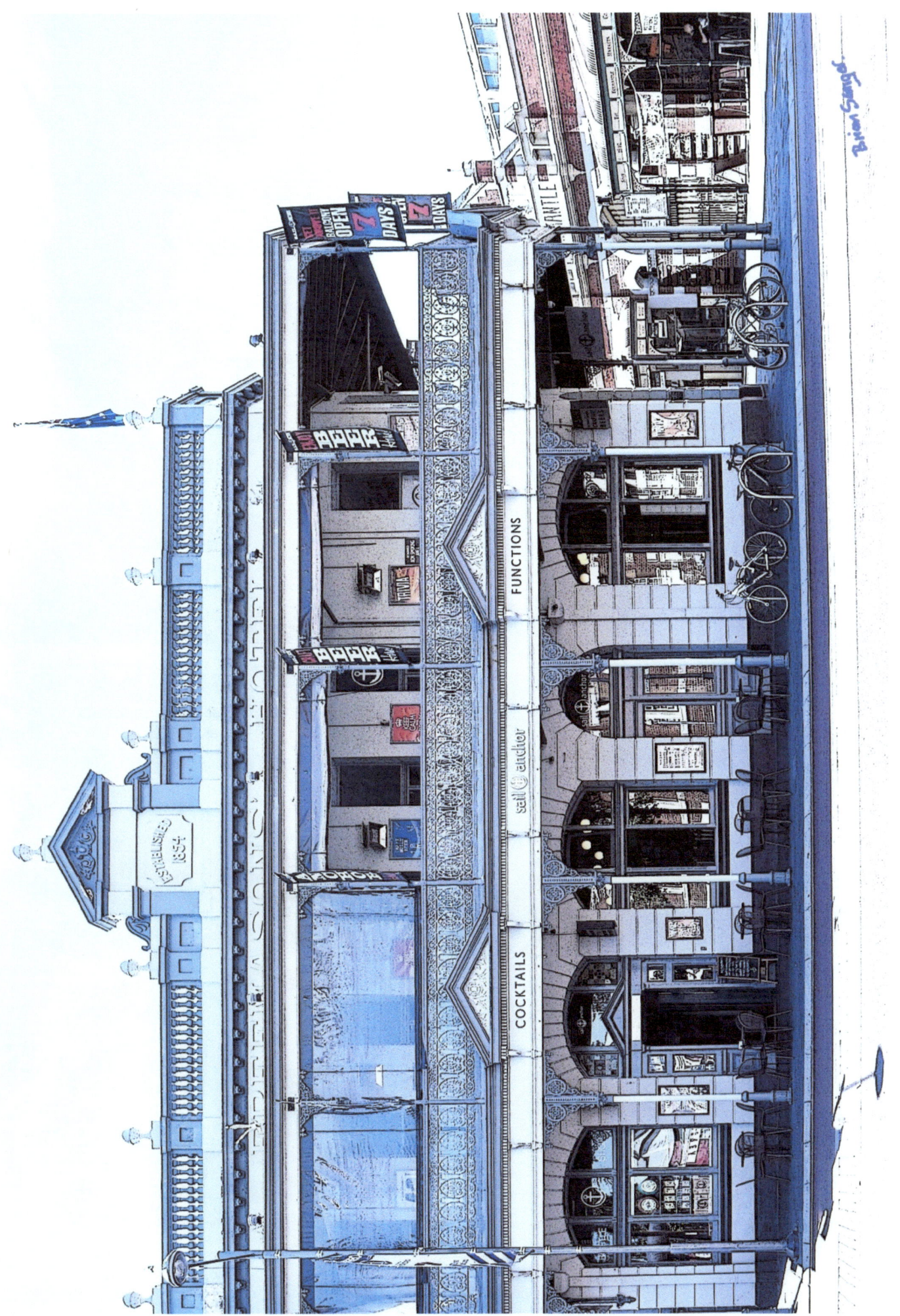

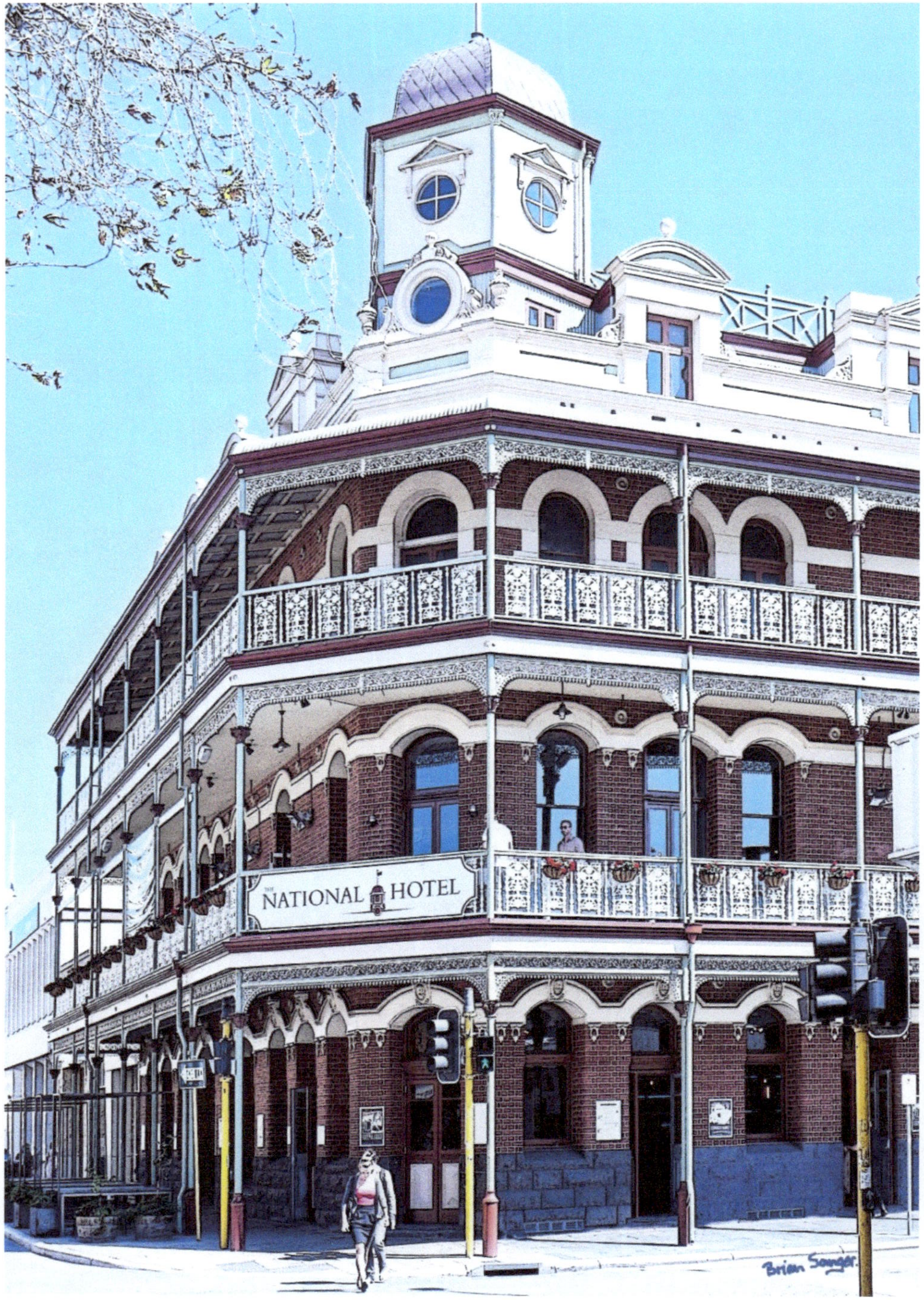
THE NATIONAL HOTEL
Brian Sanger

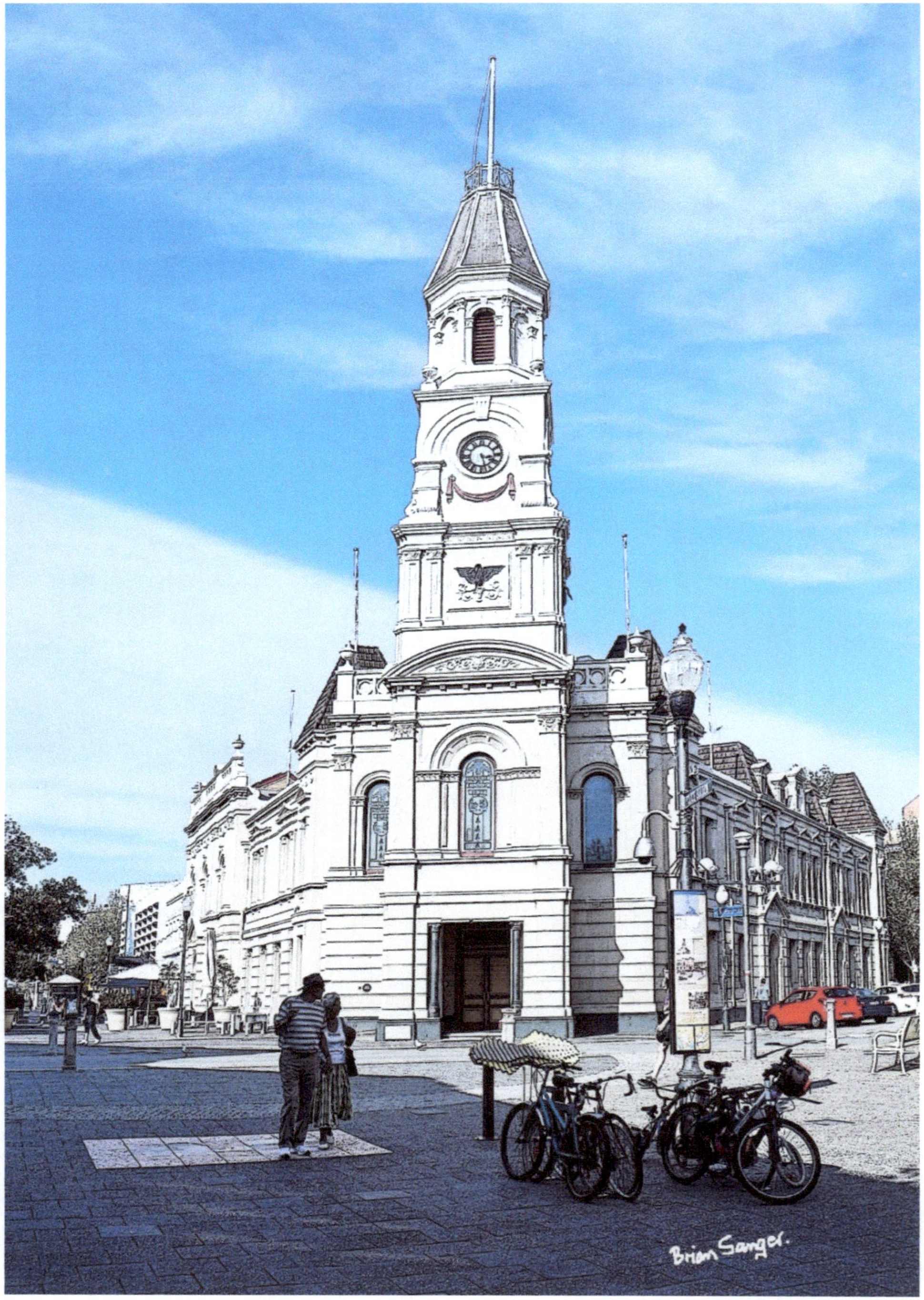
Brian Sanger.

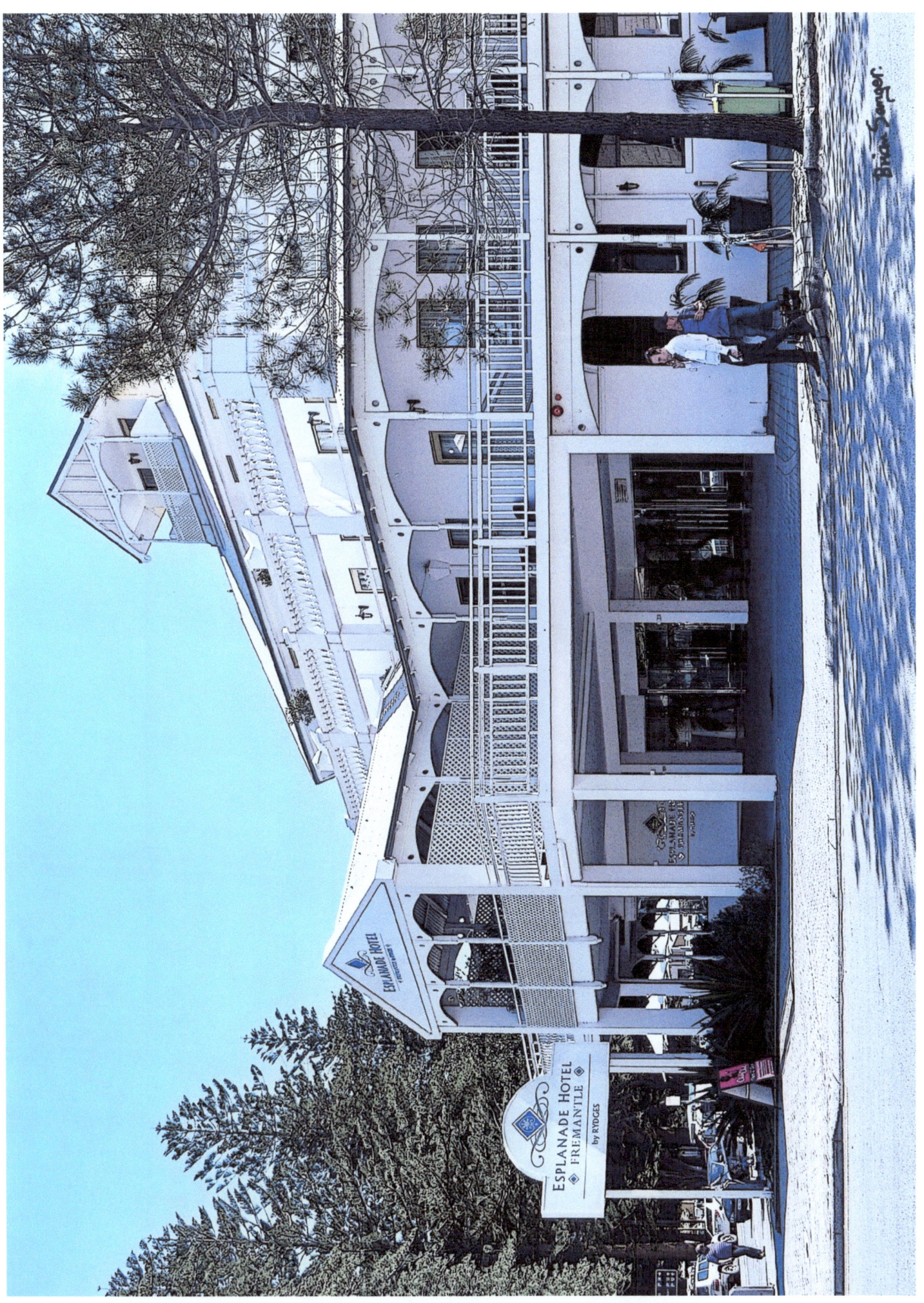

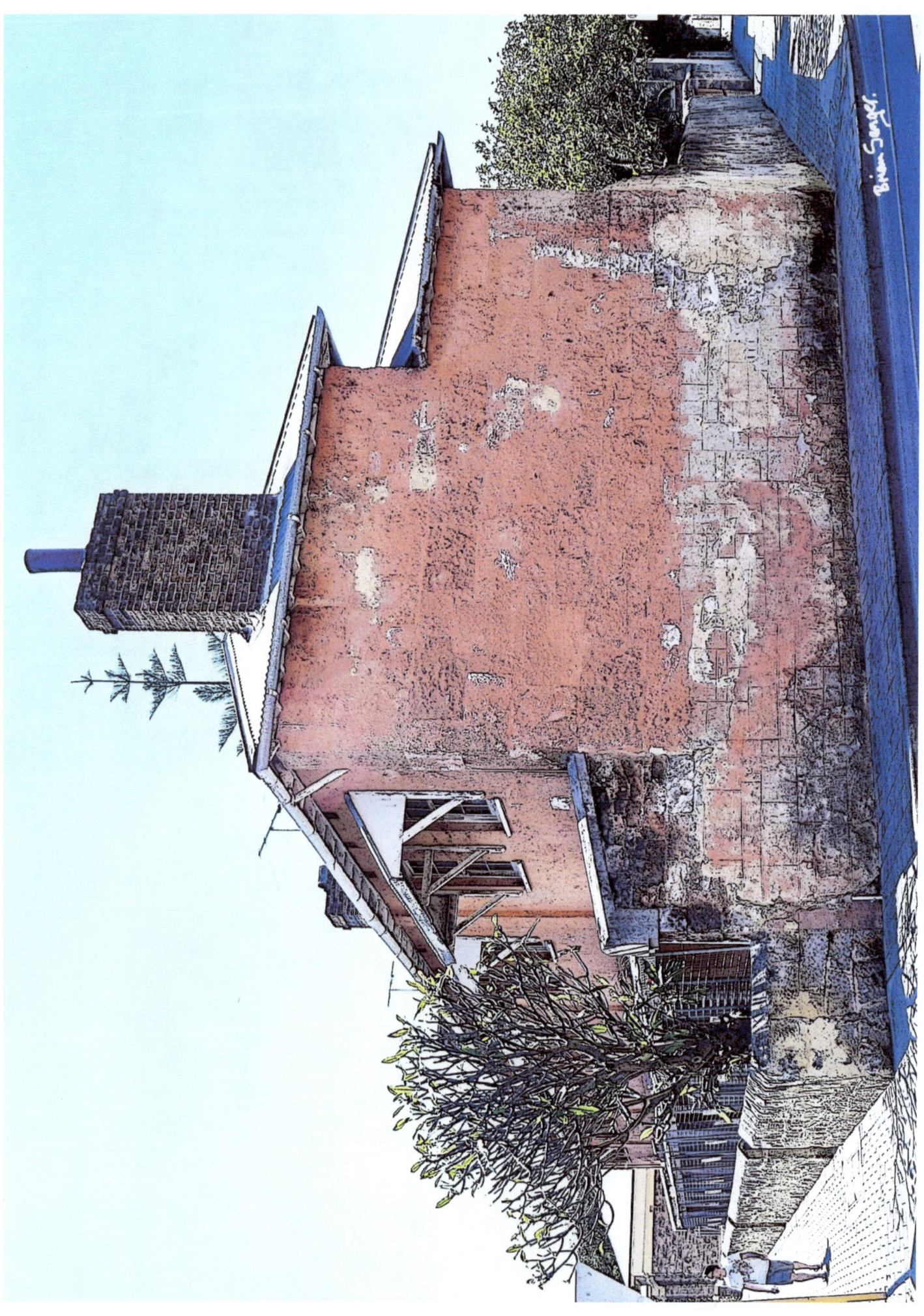

Brian Sanger.

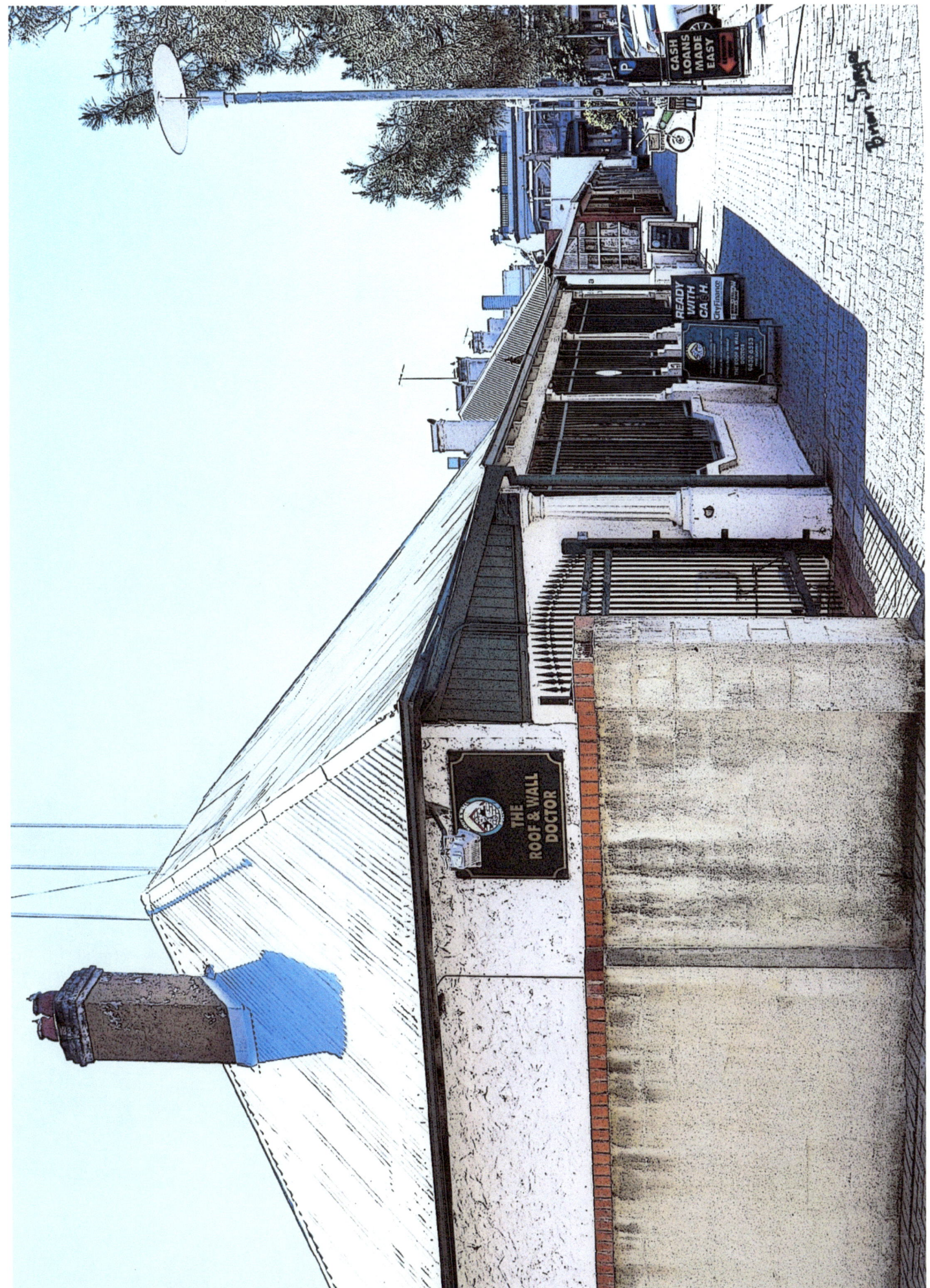

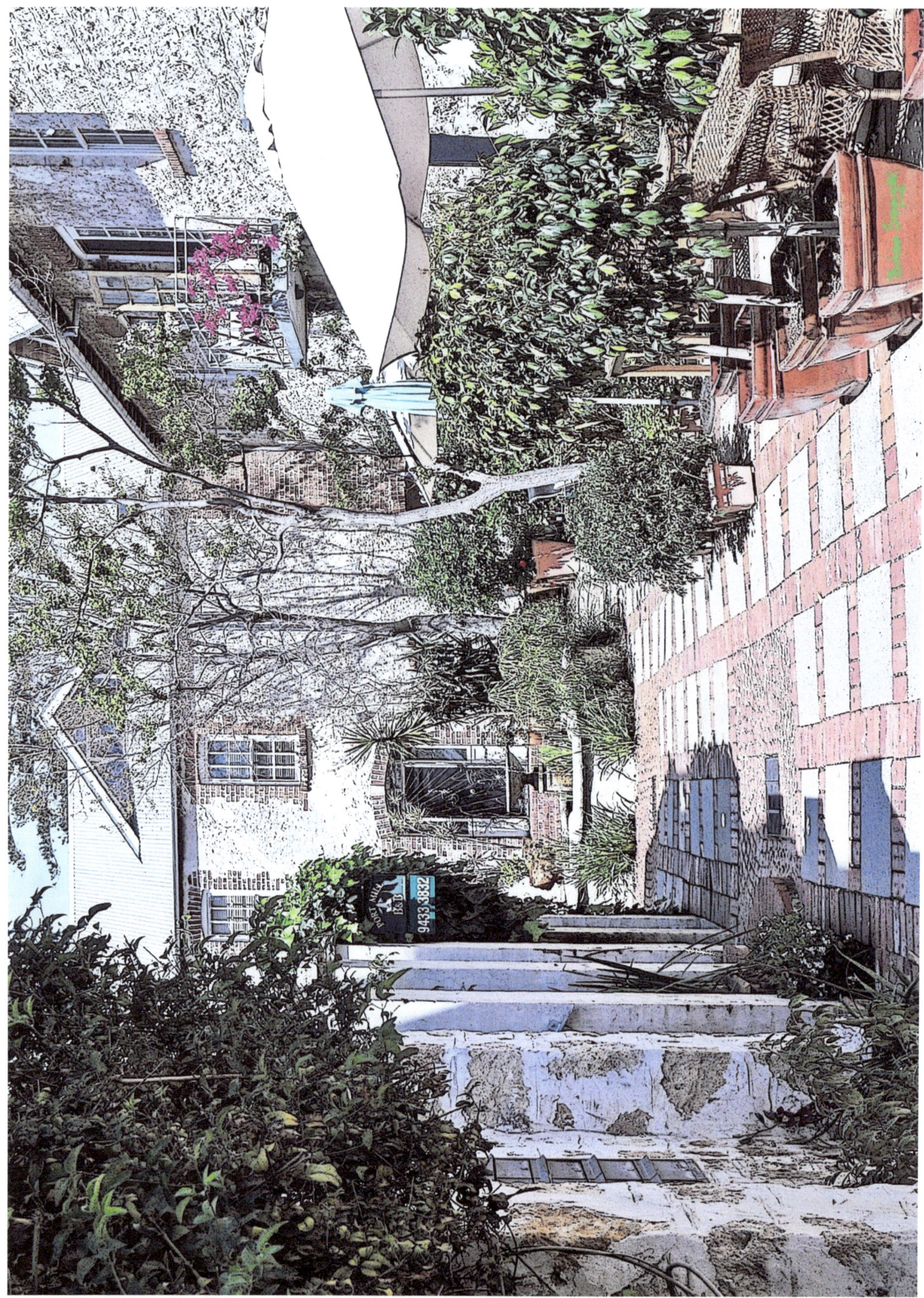

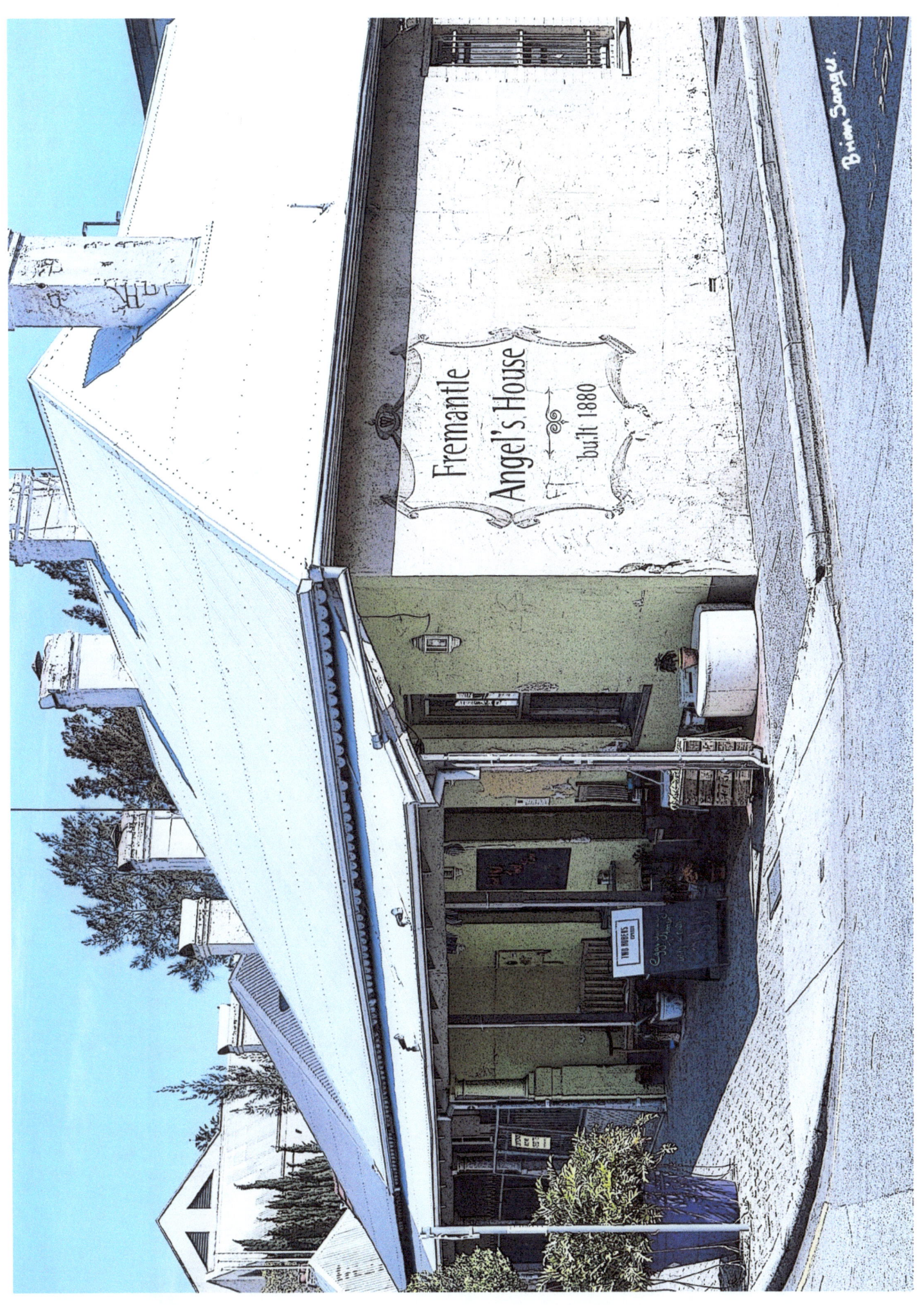

Fremantle
Angel's House
built 1880

Brian Sarger.

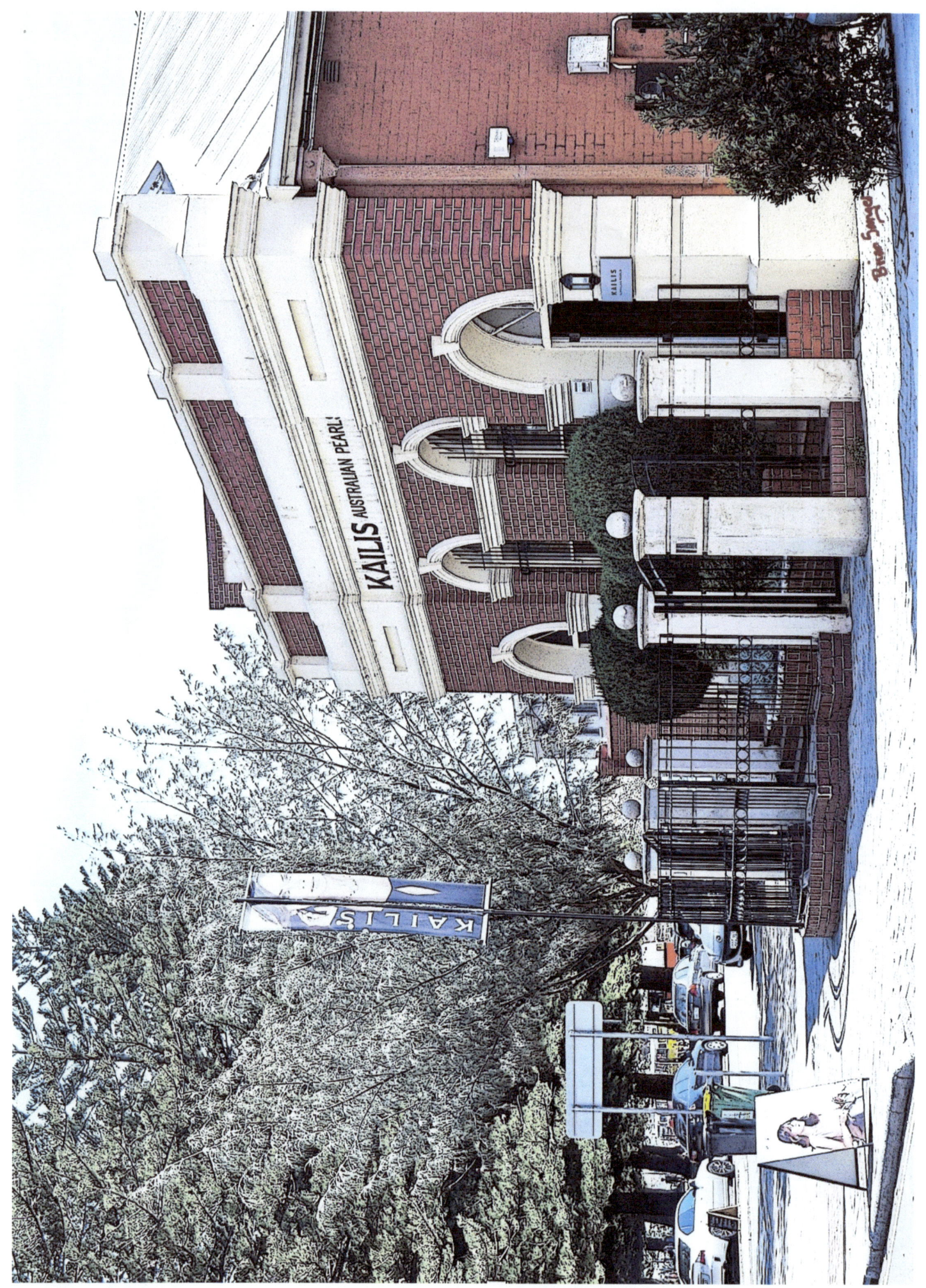

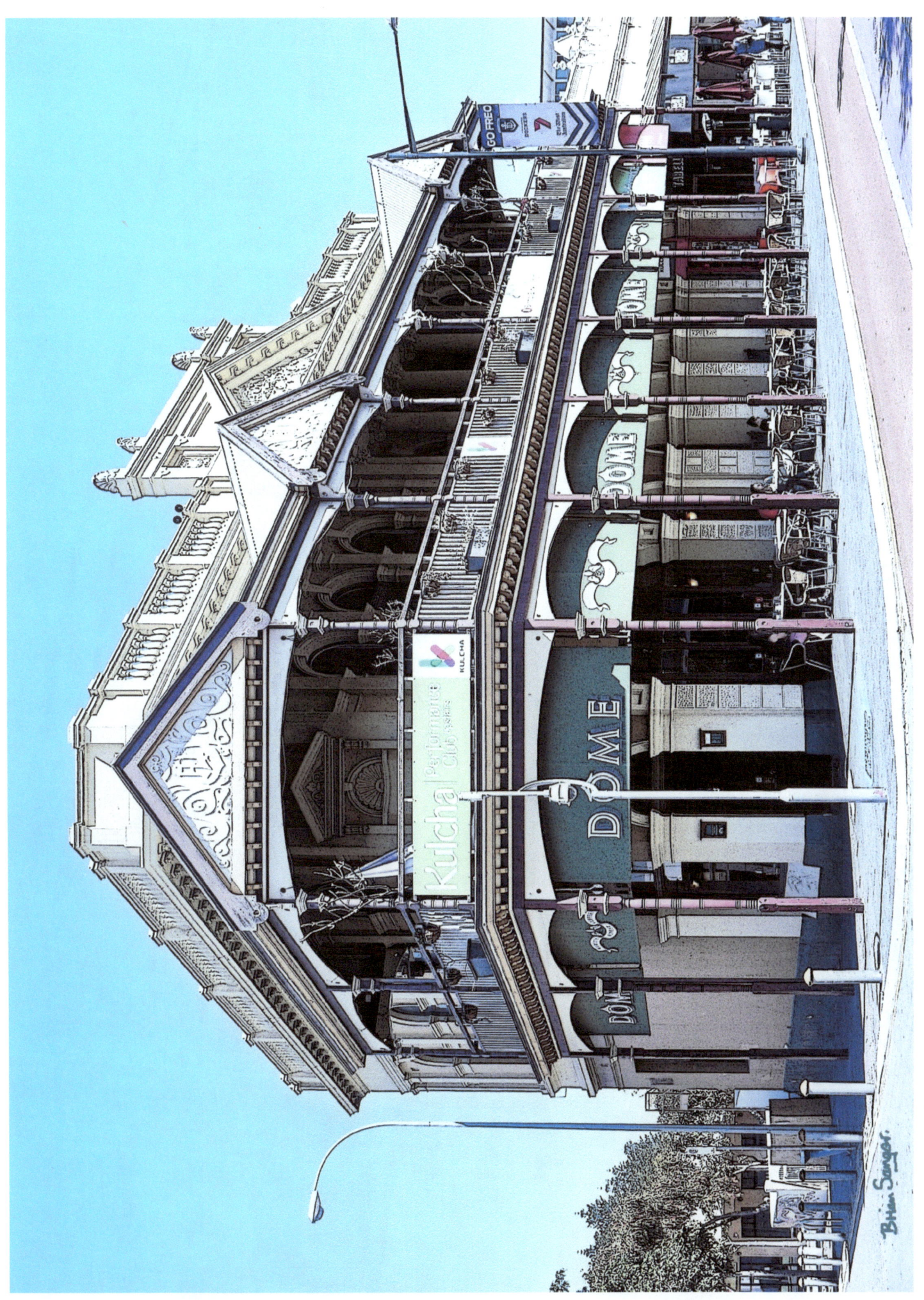

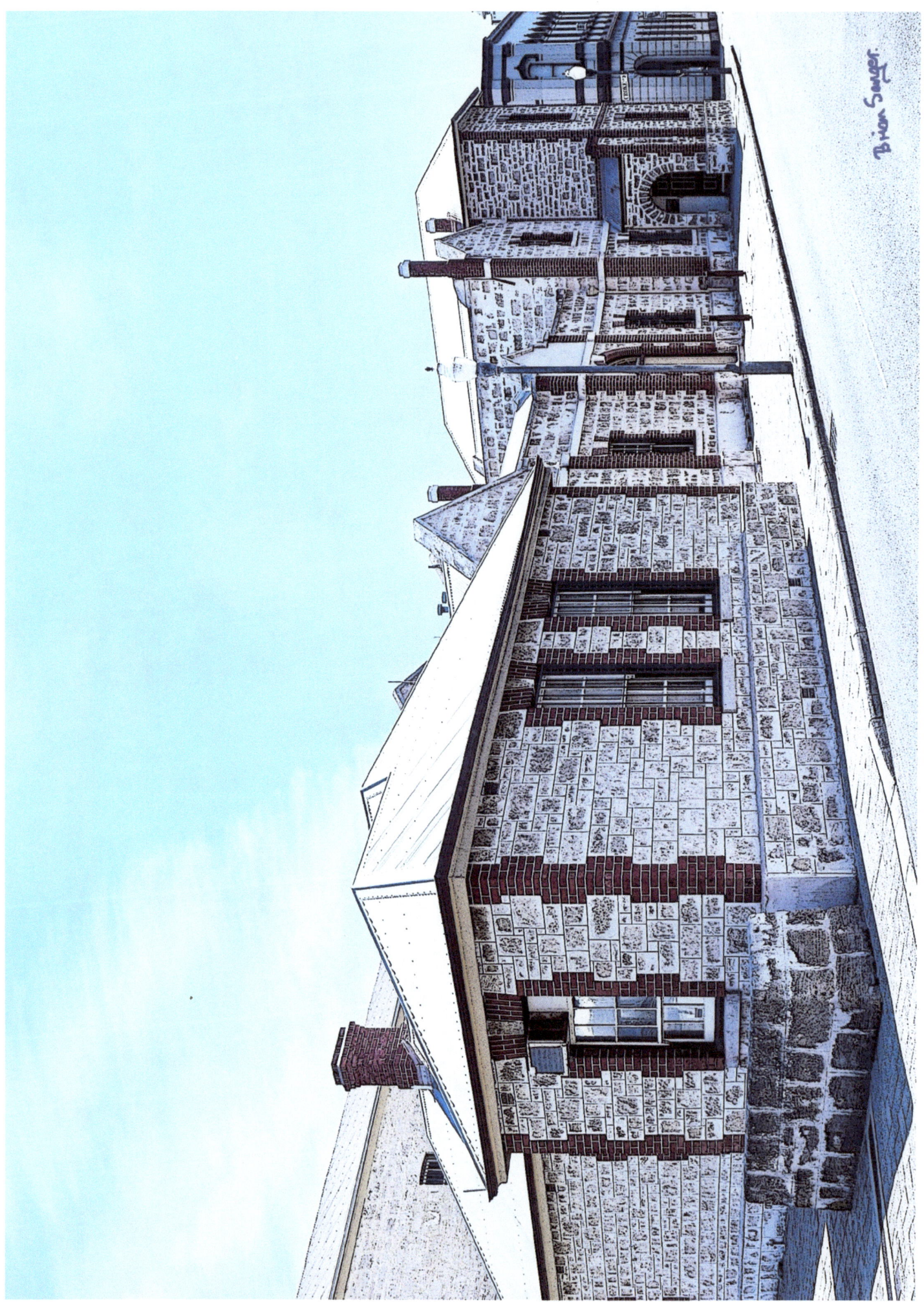

Brian Sauer.

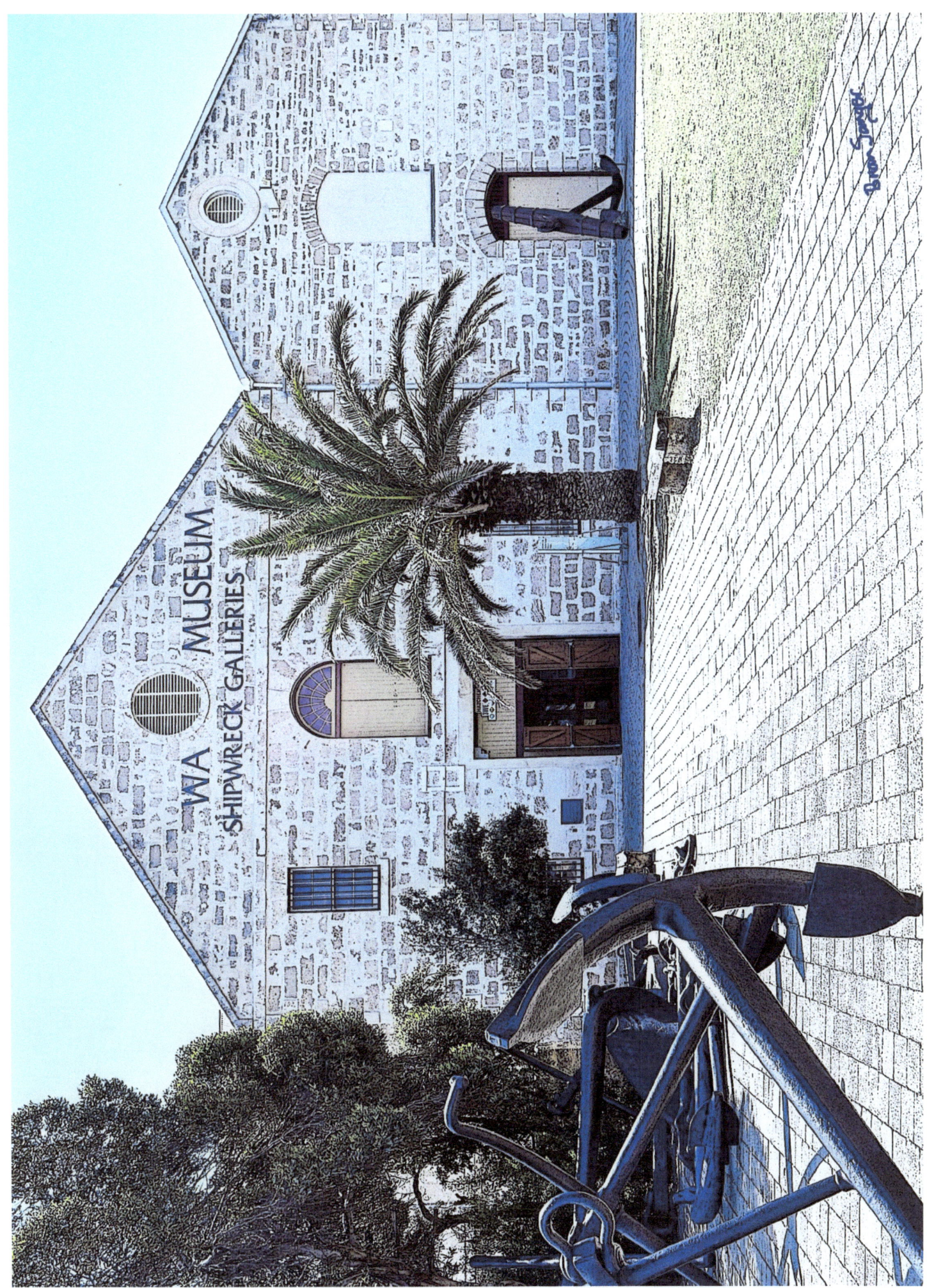

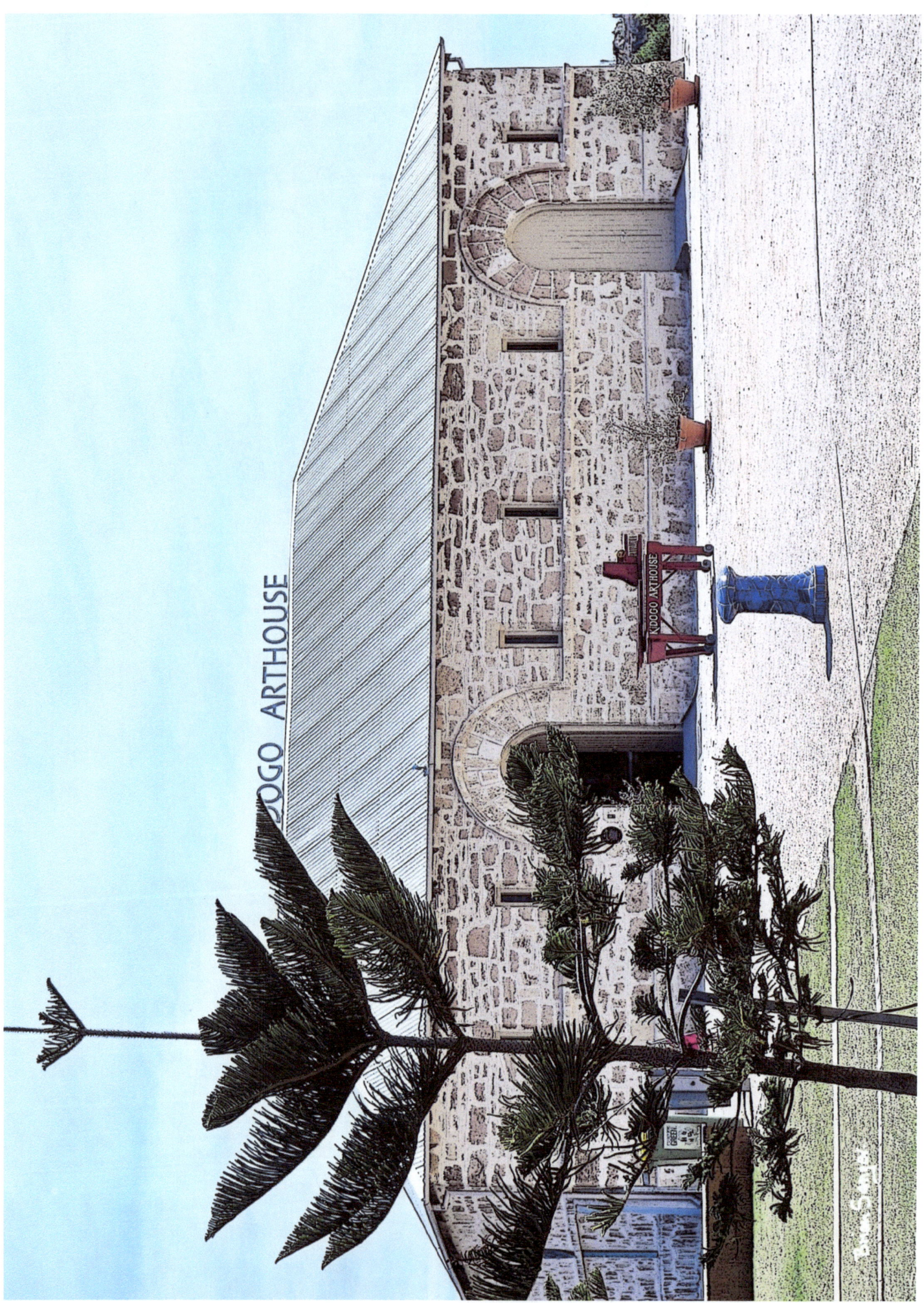

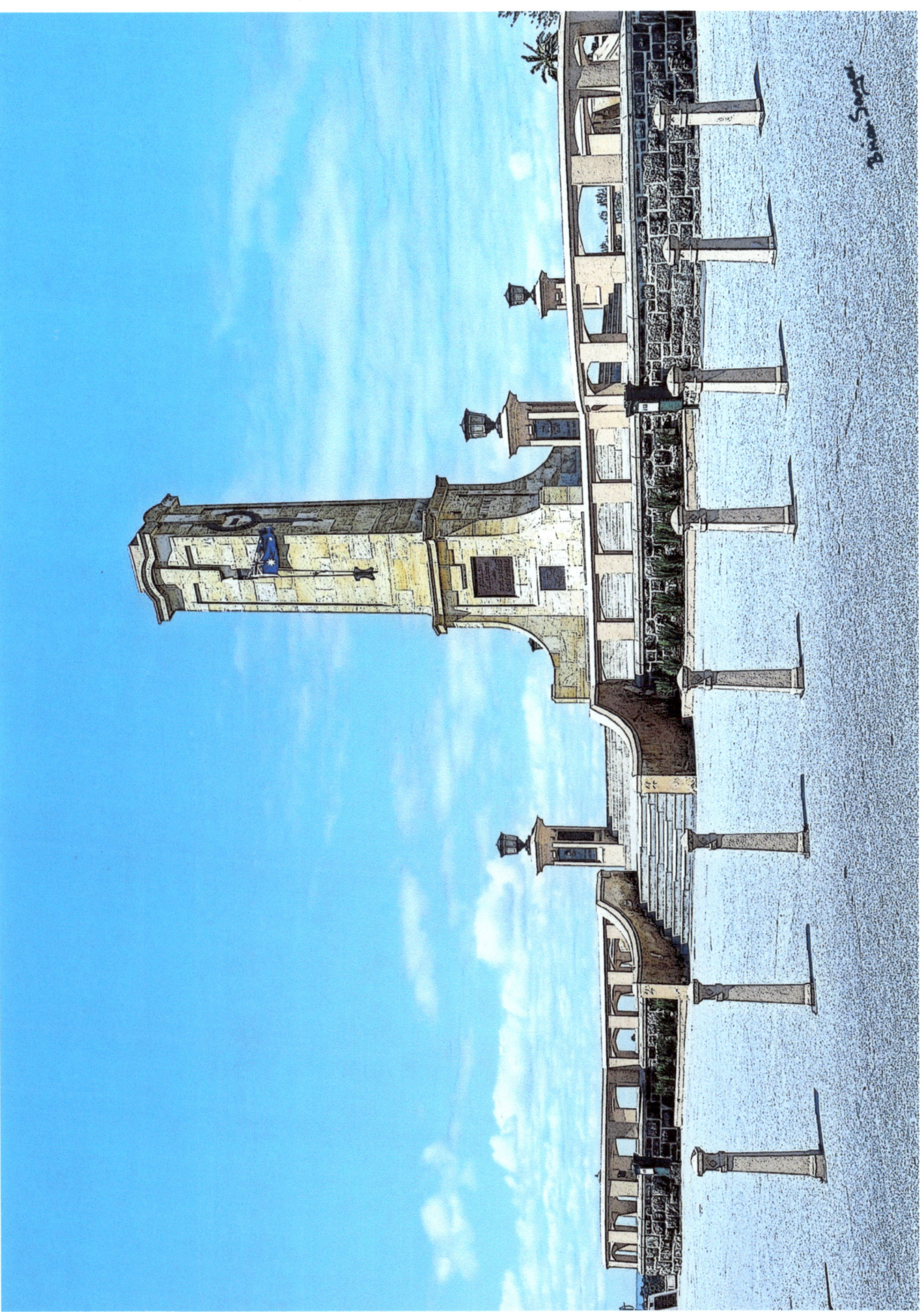

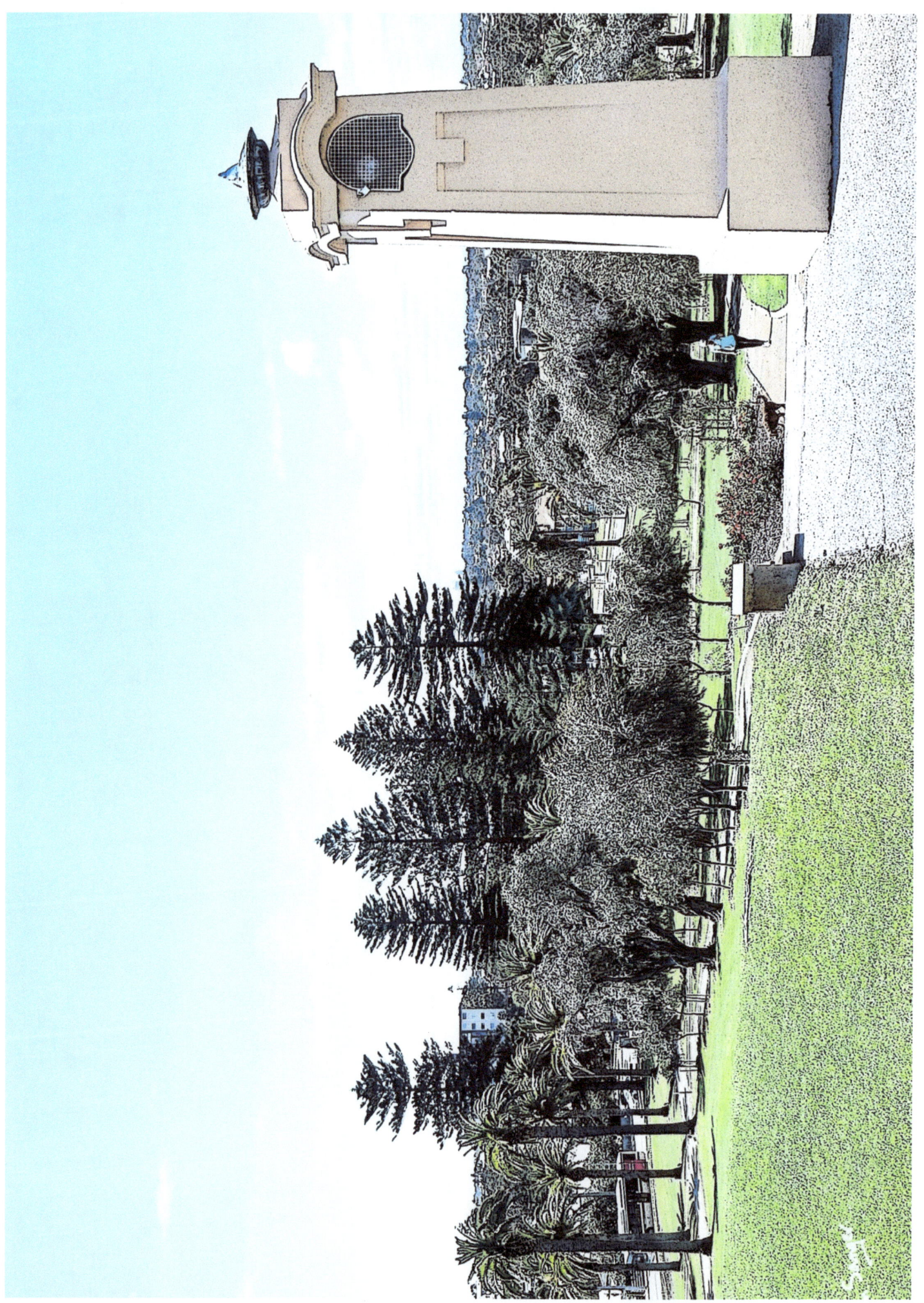

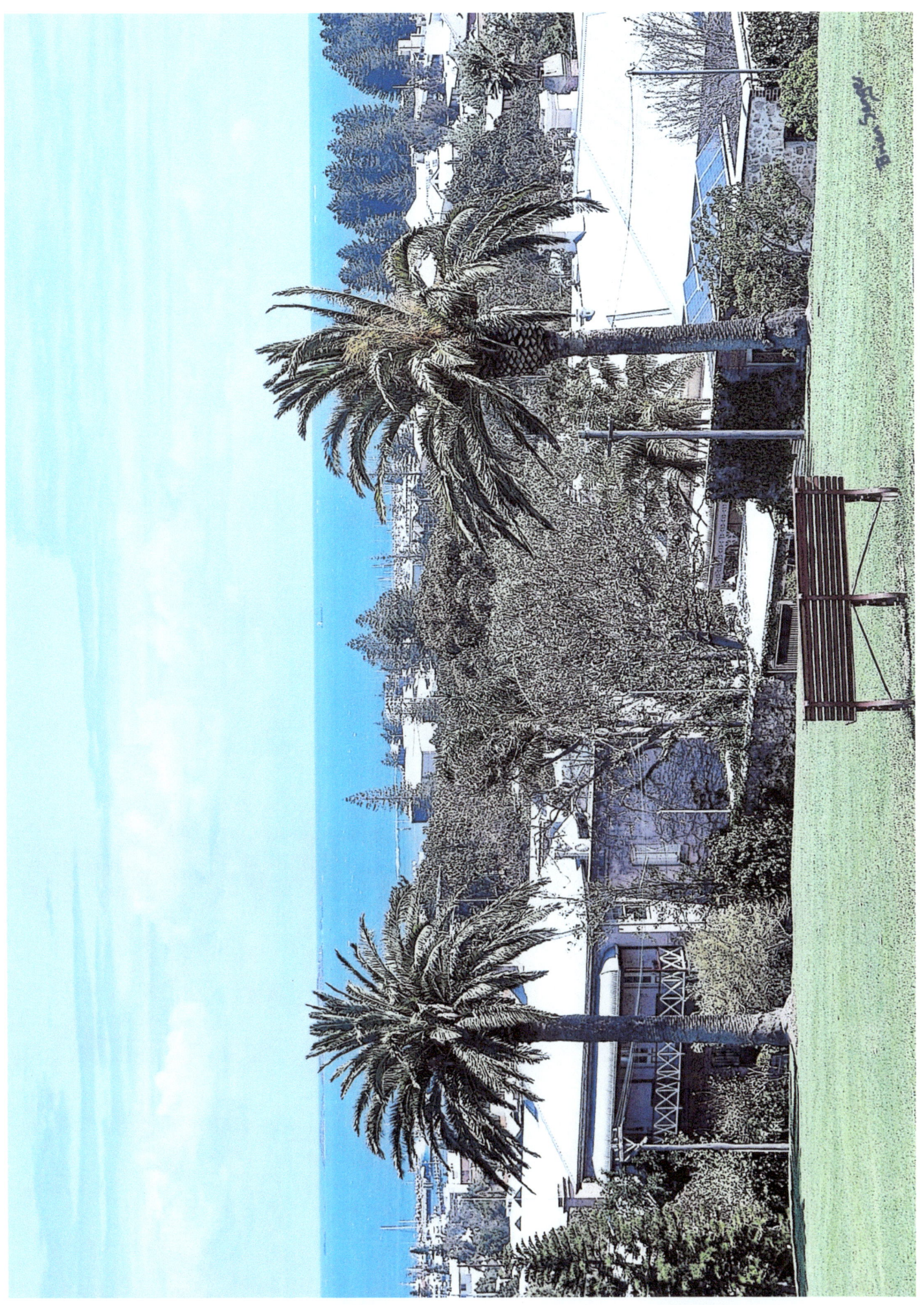

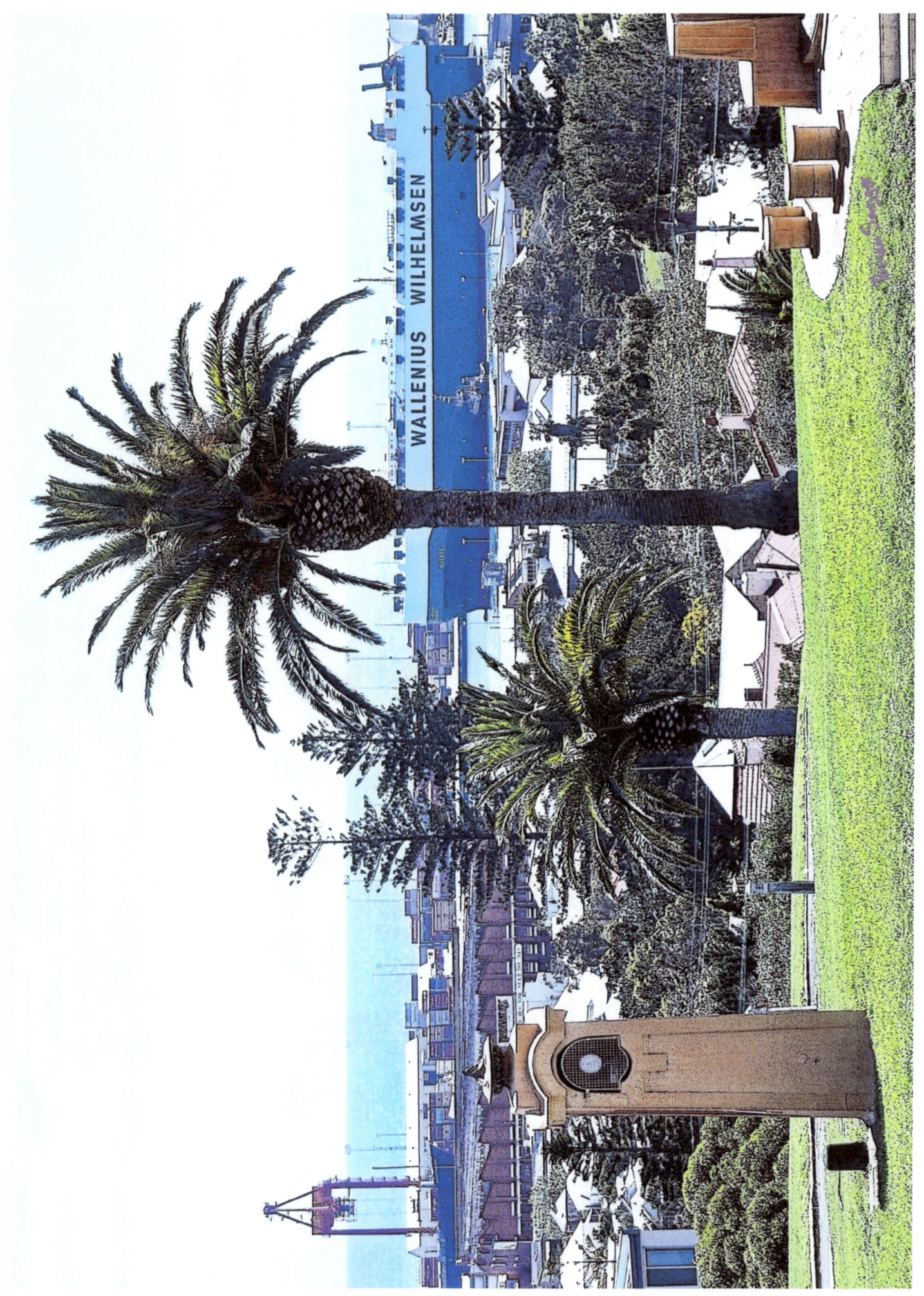

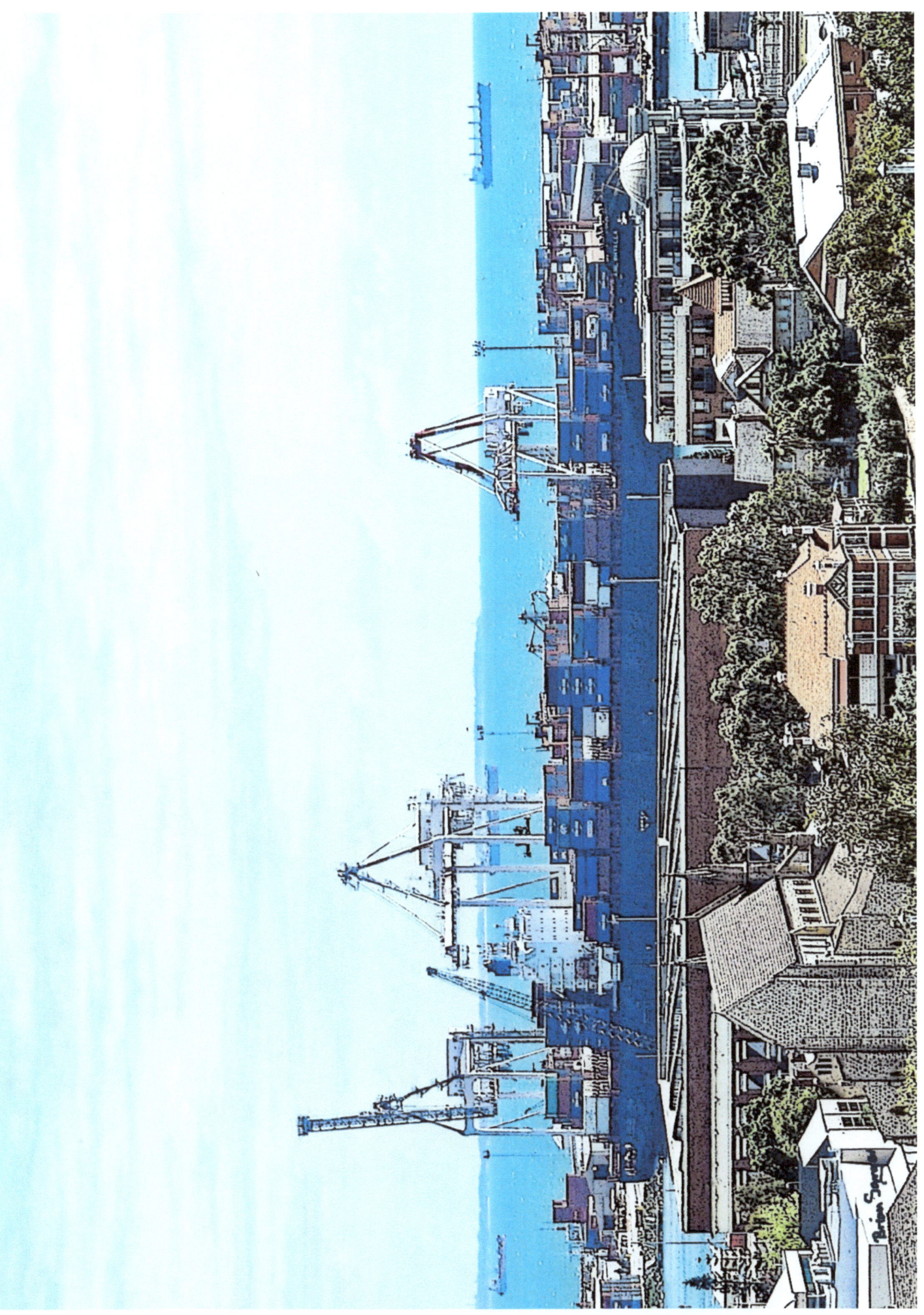

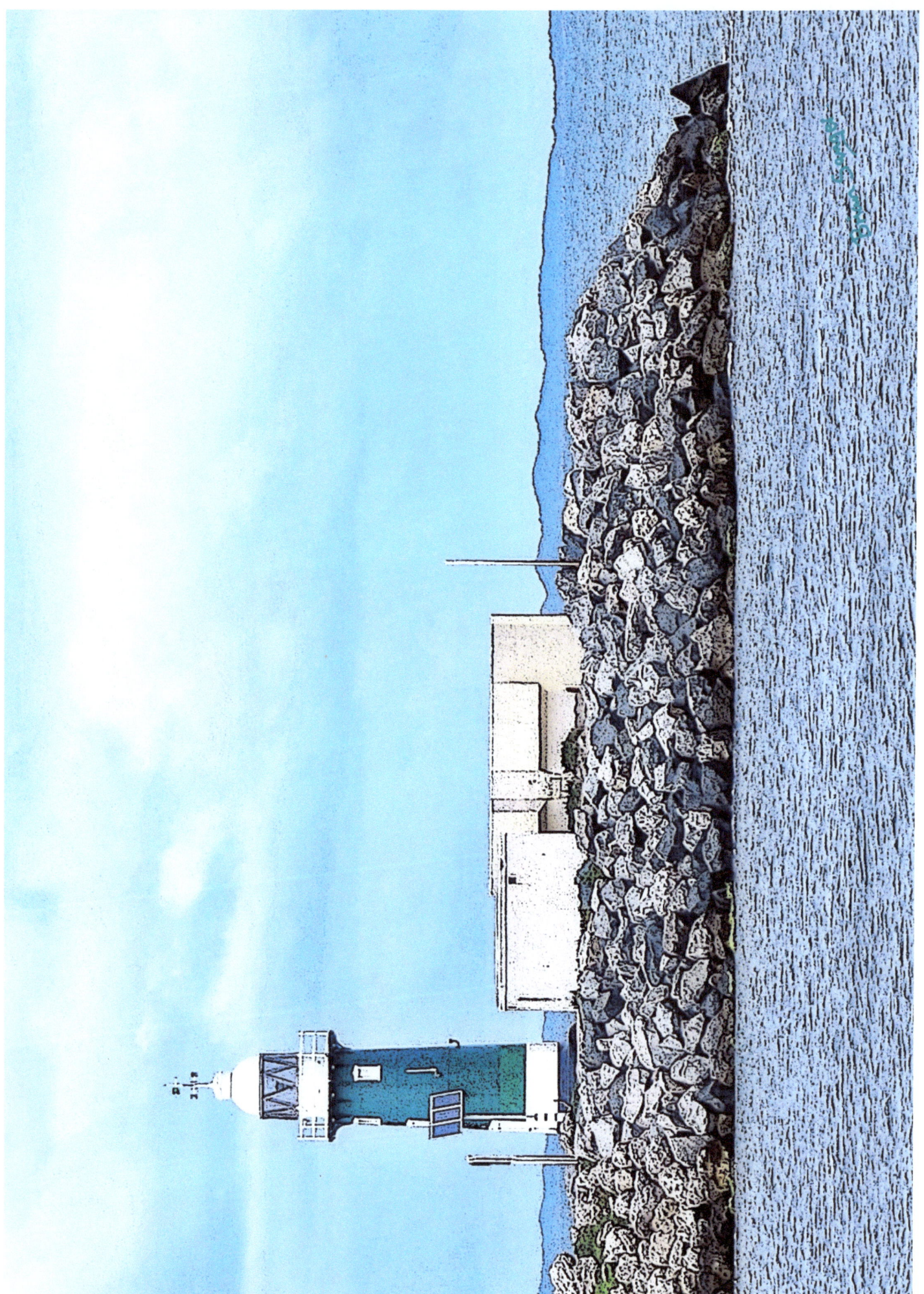

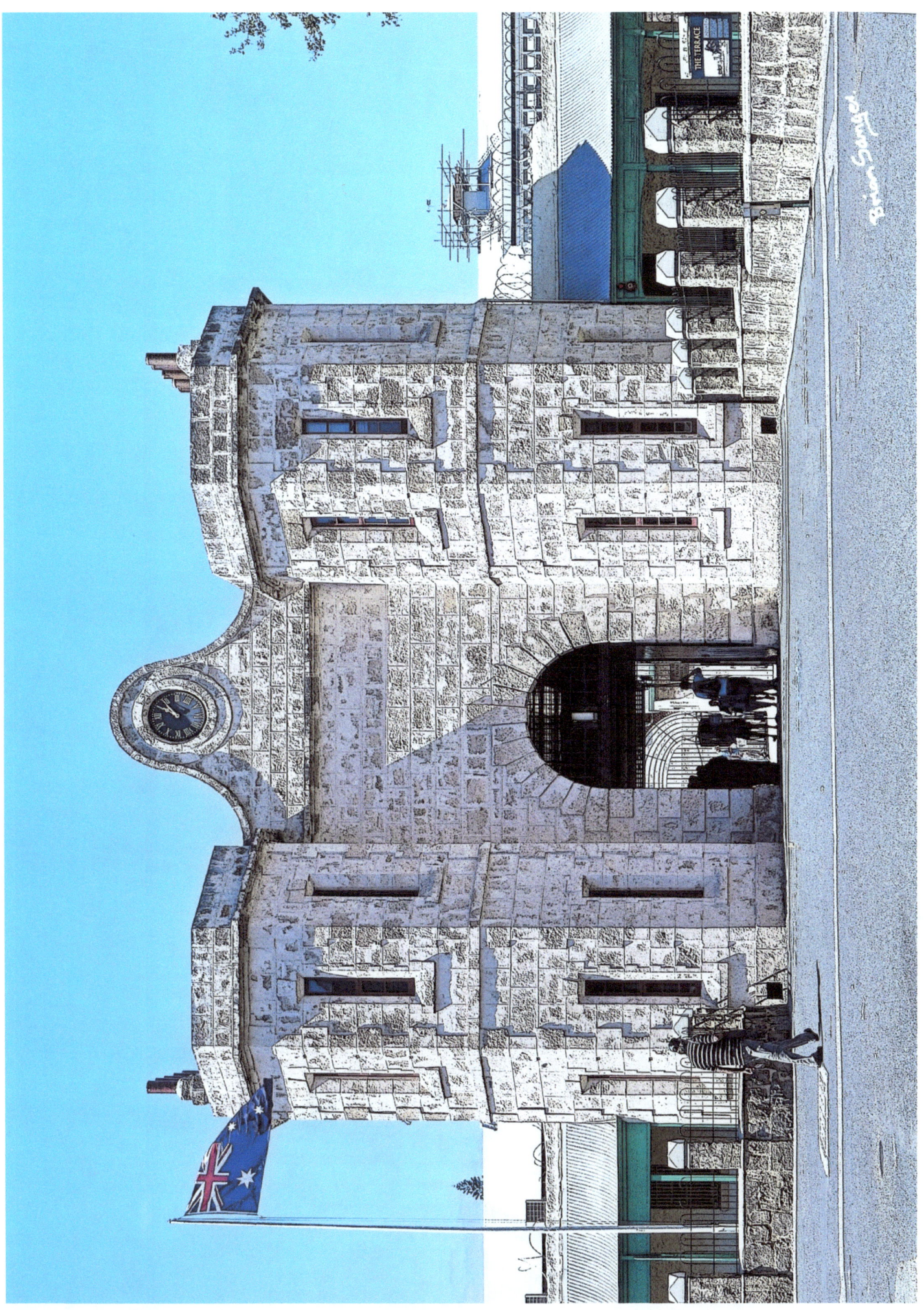

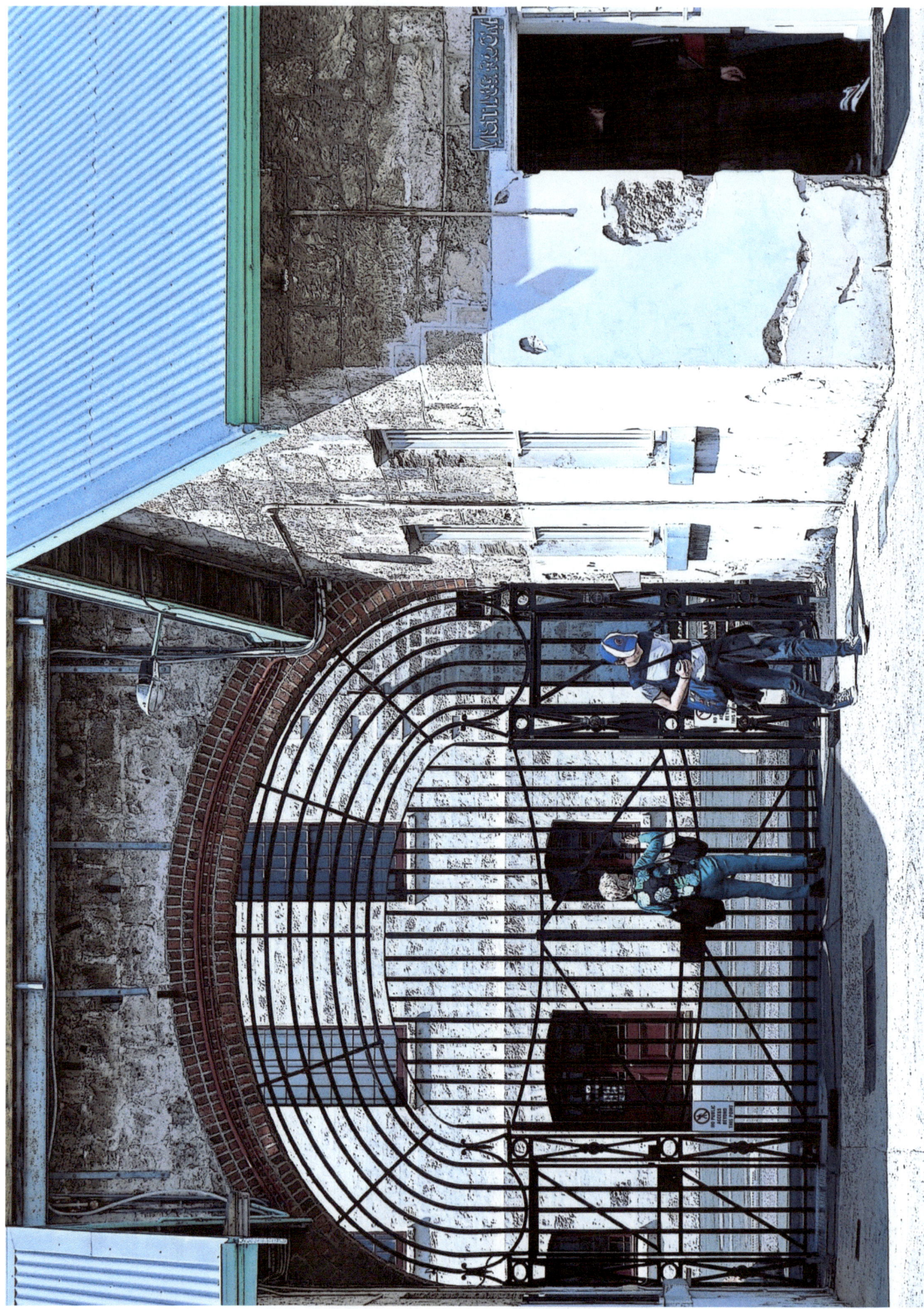

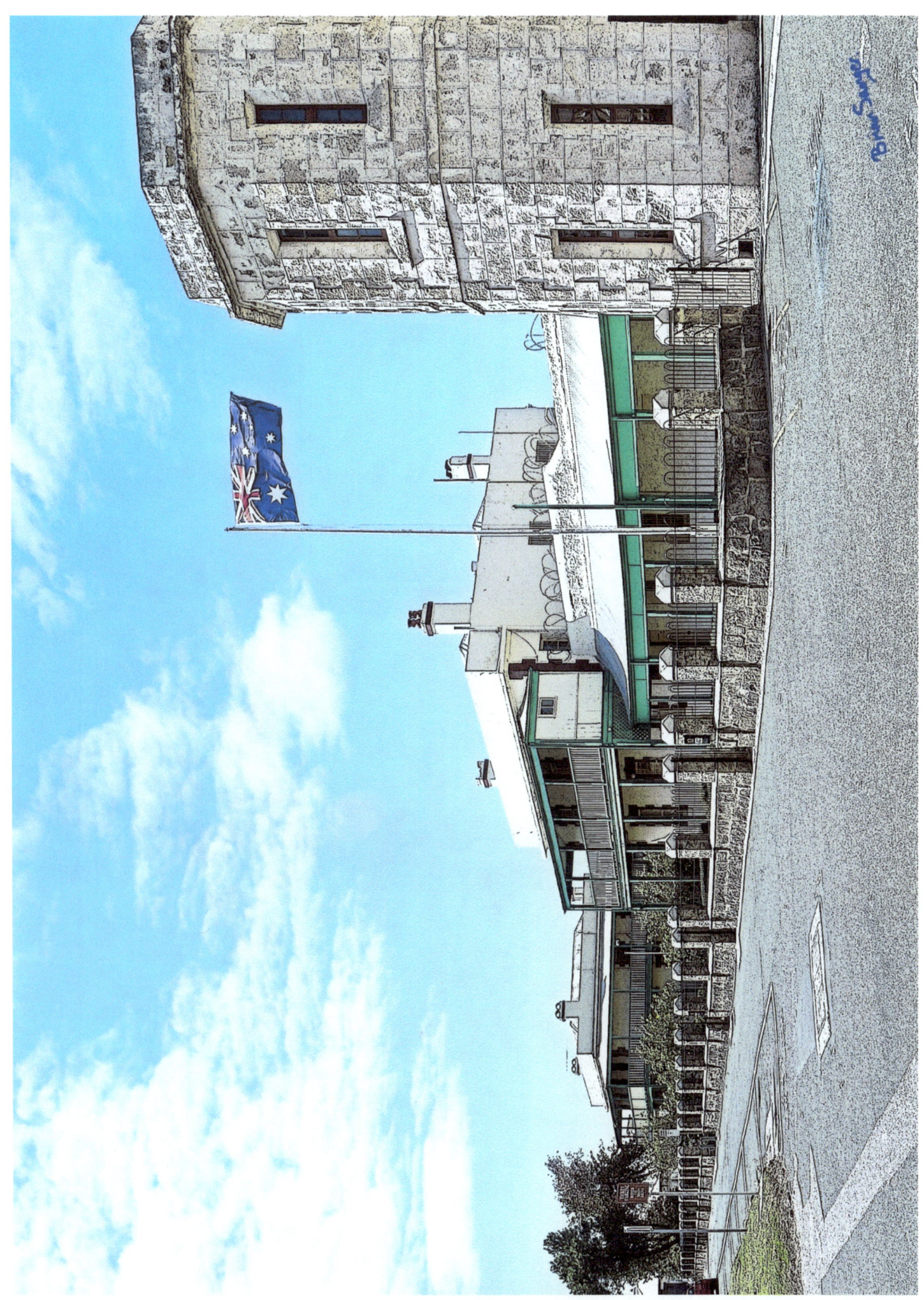

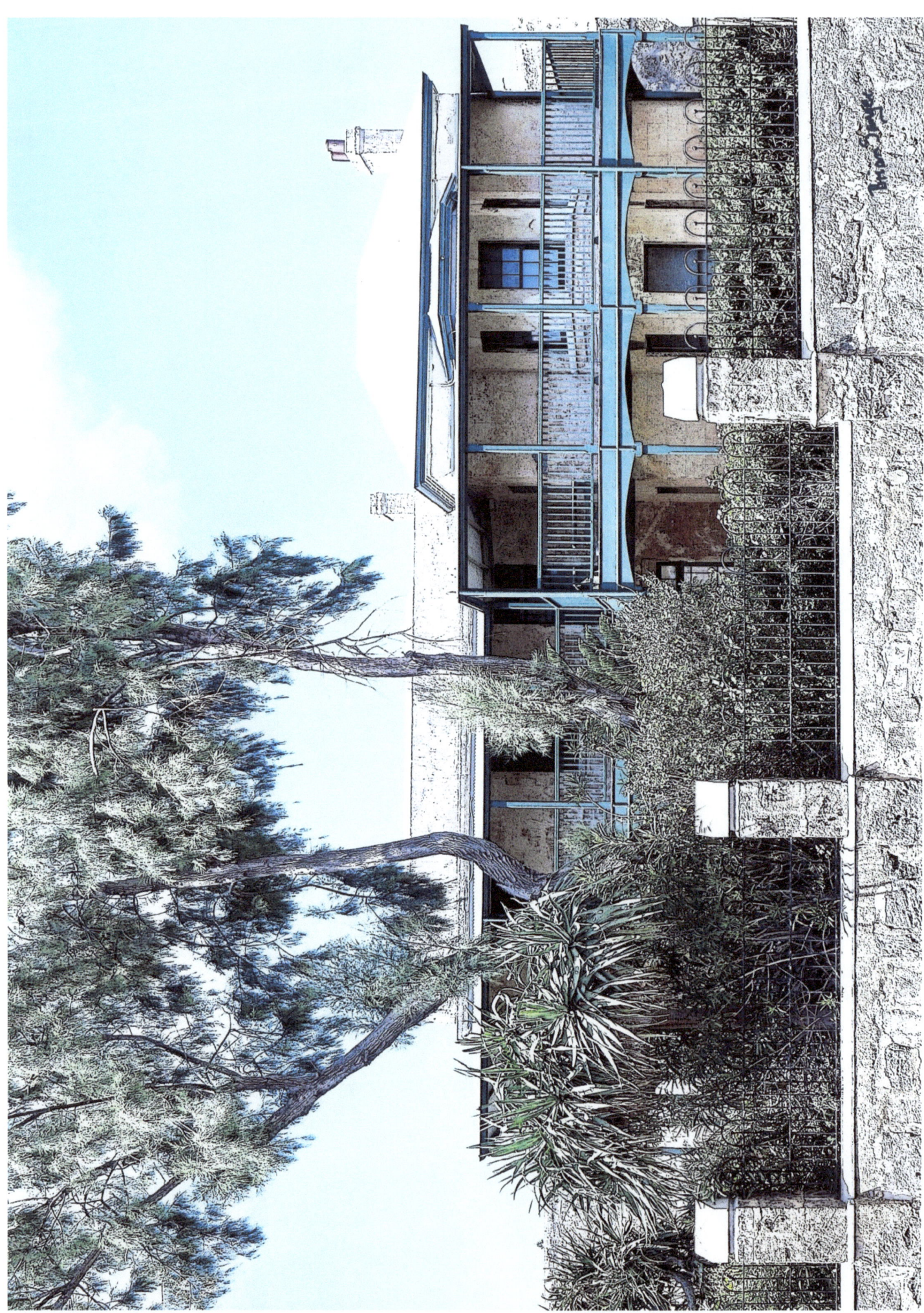

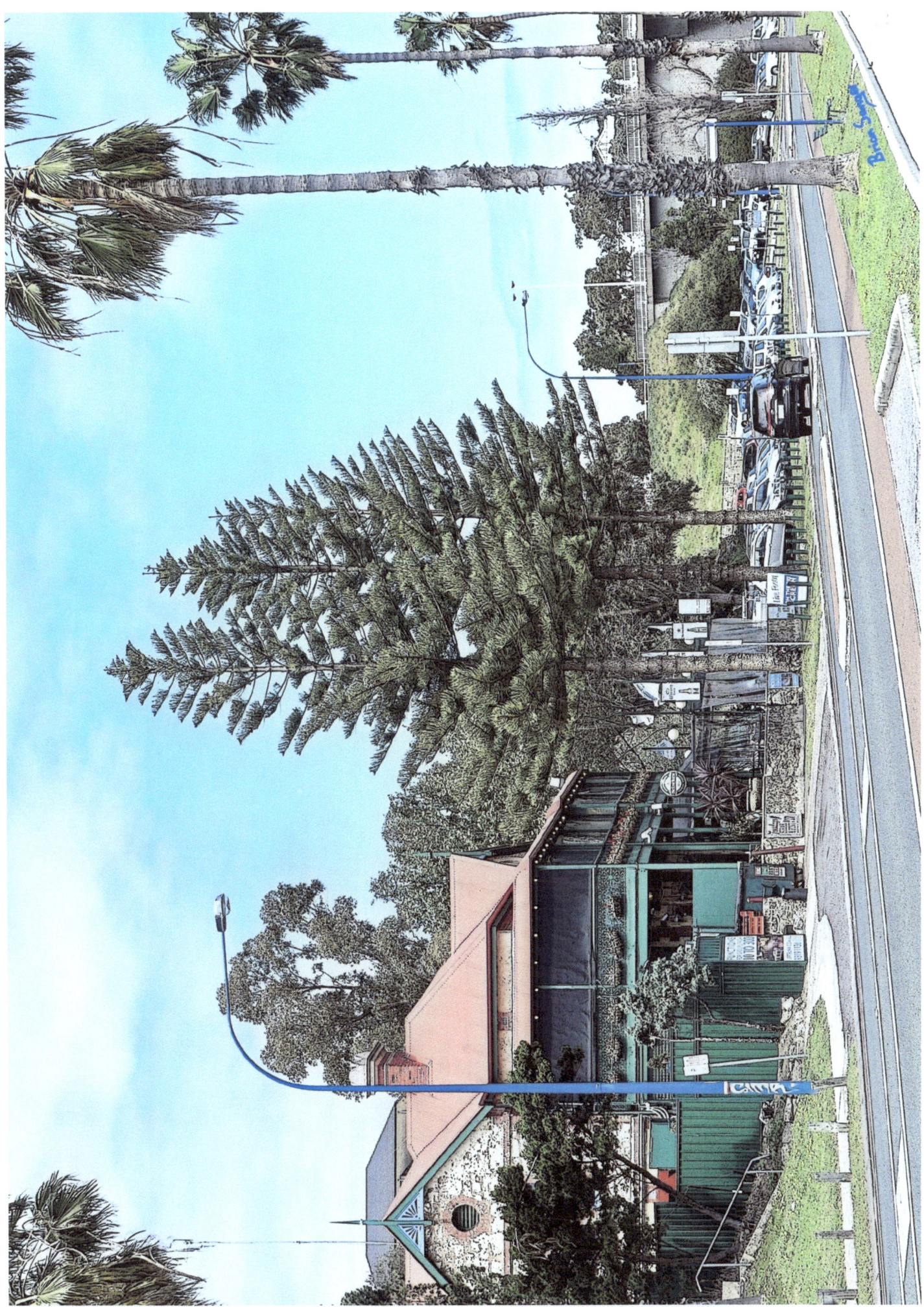

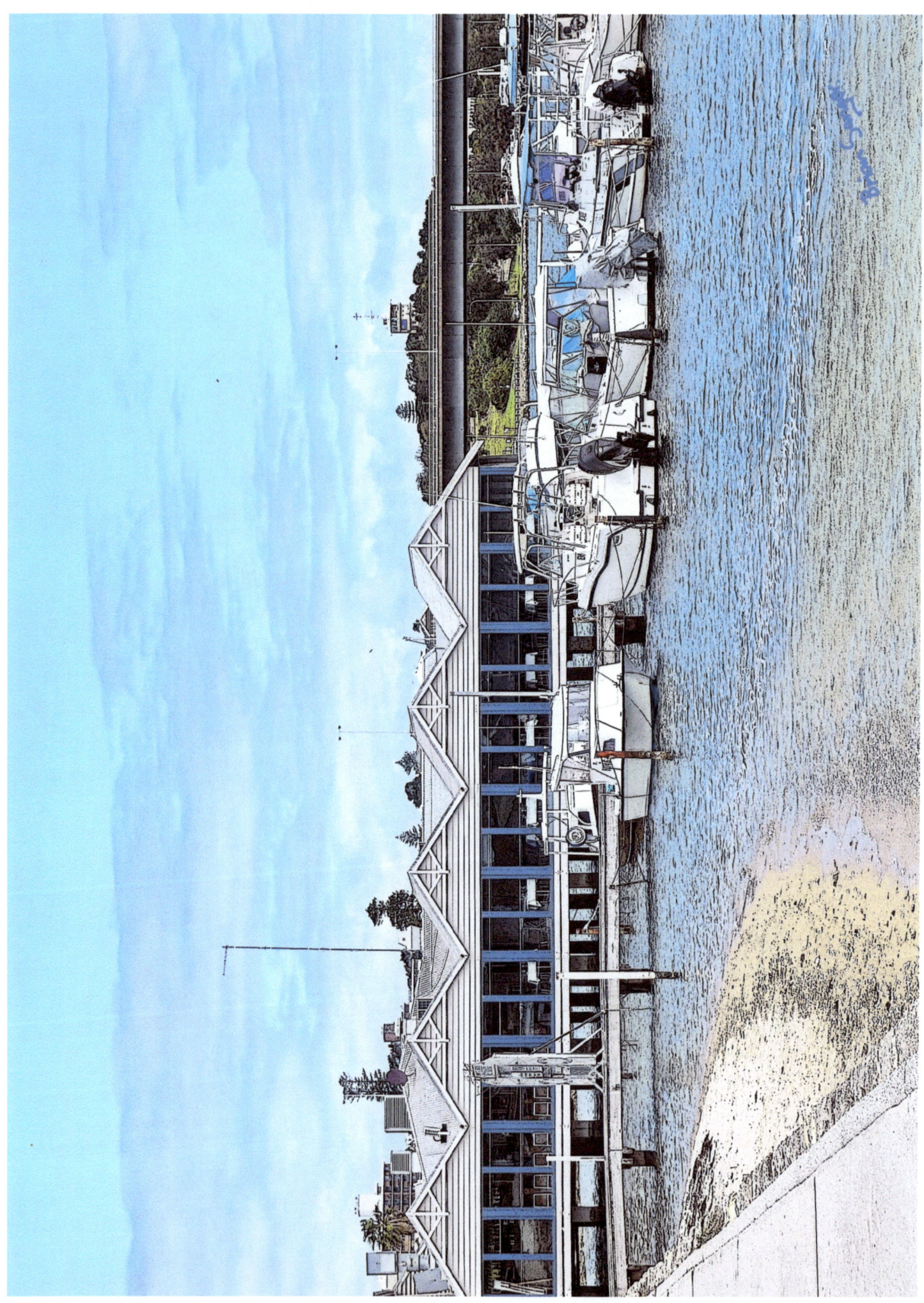

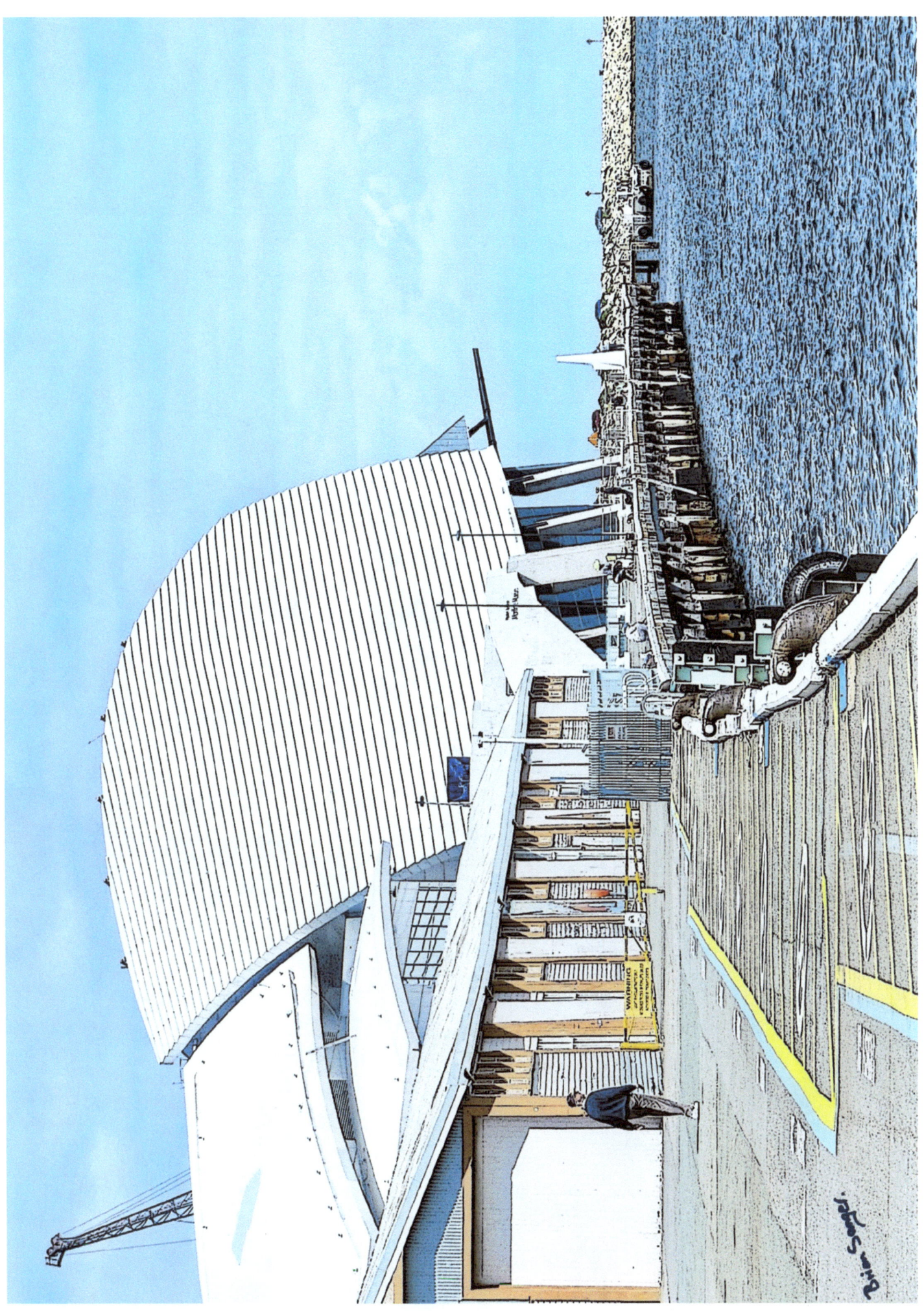

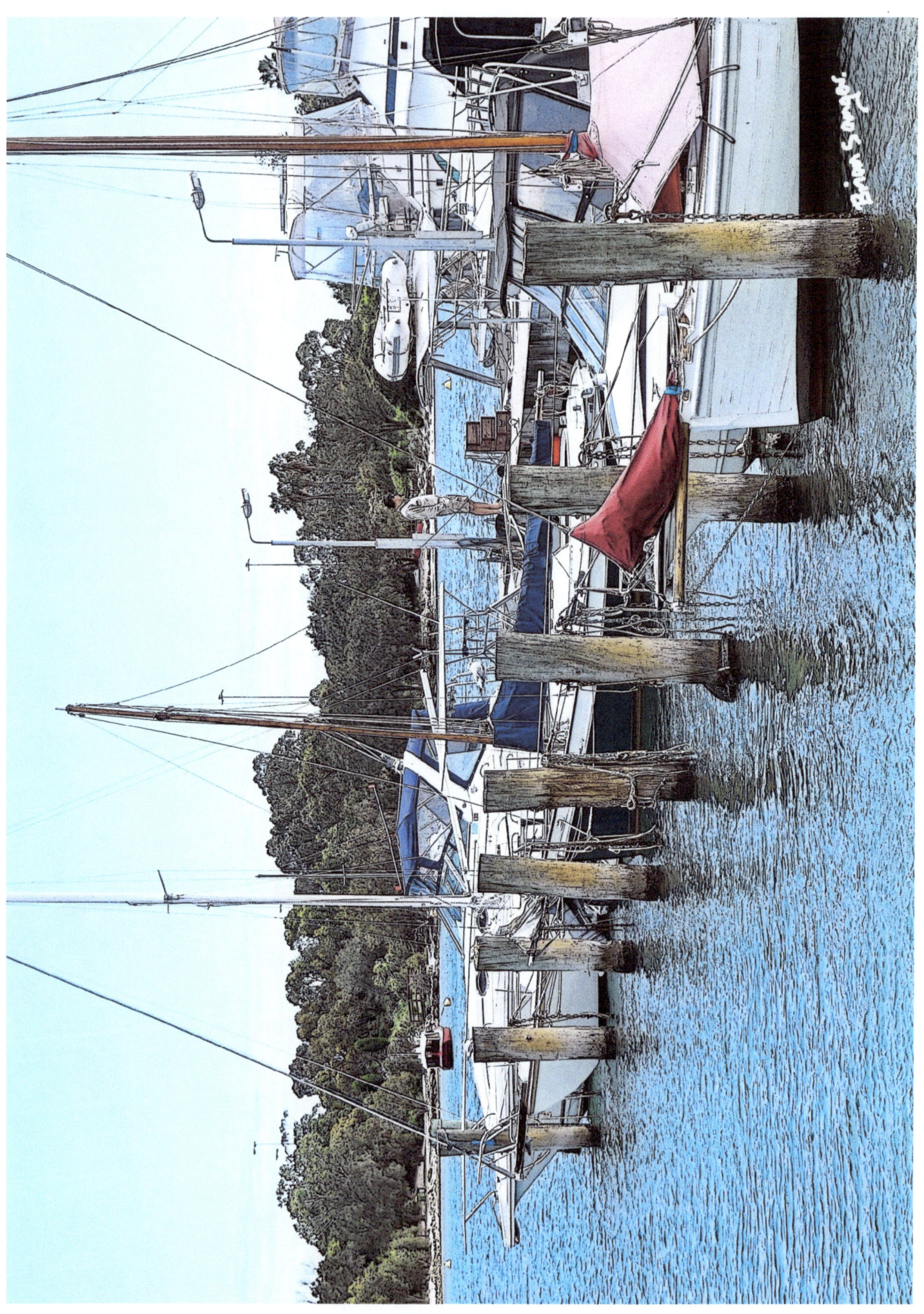

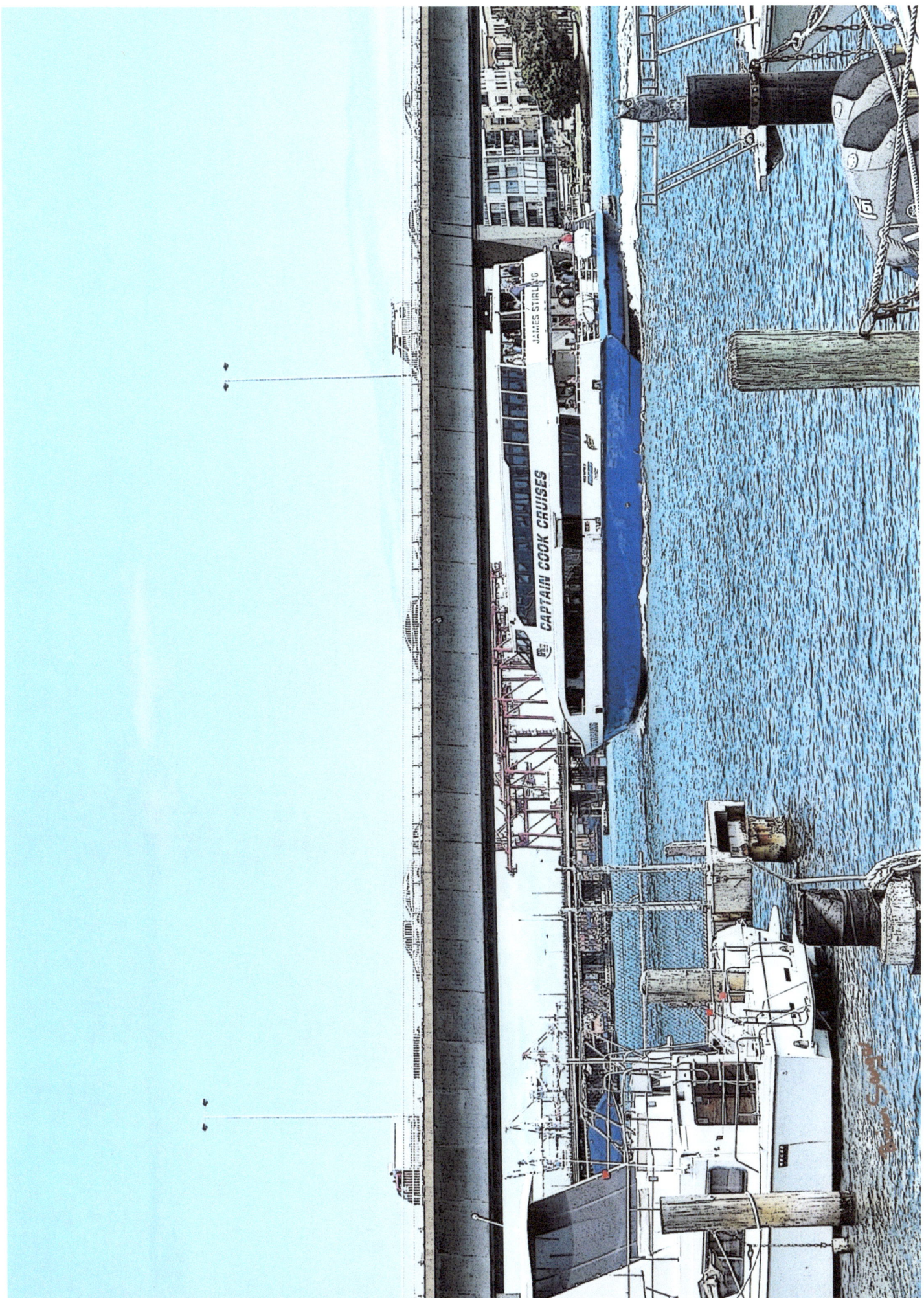

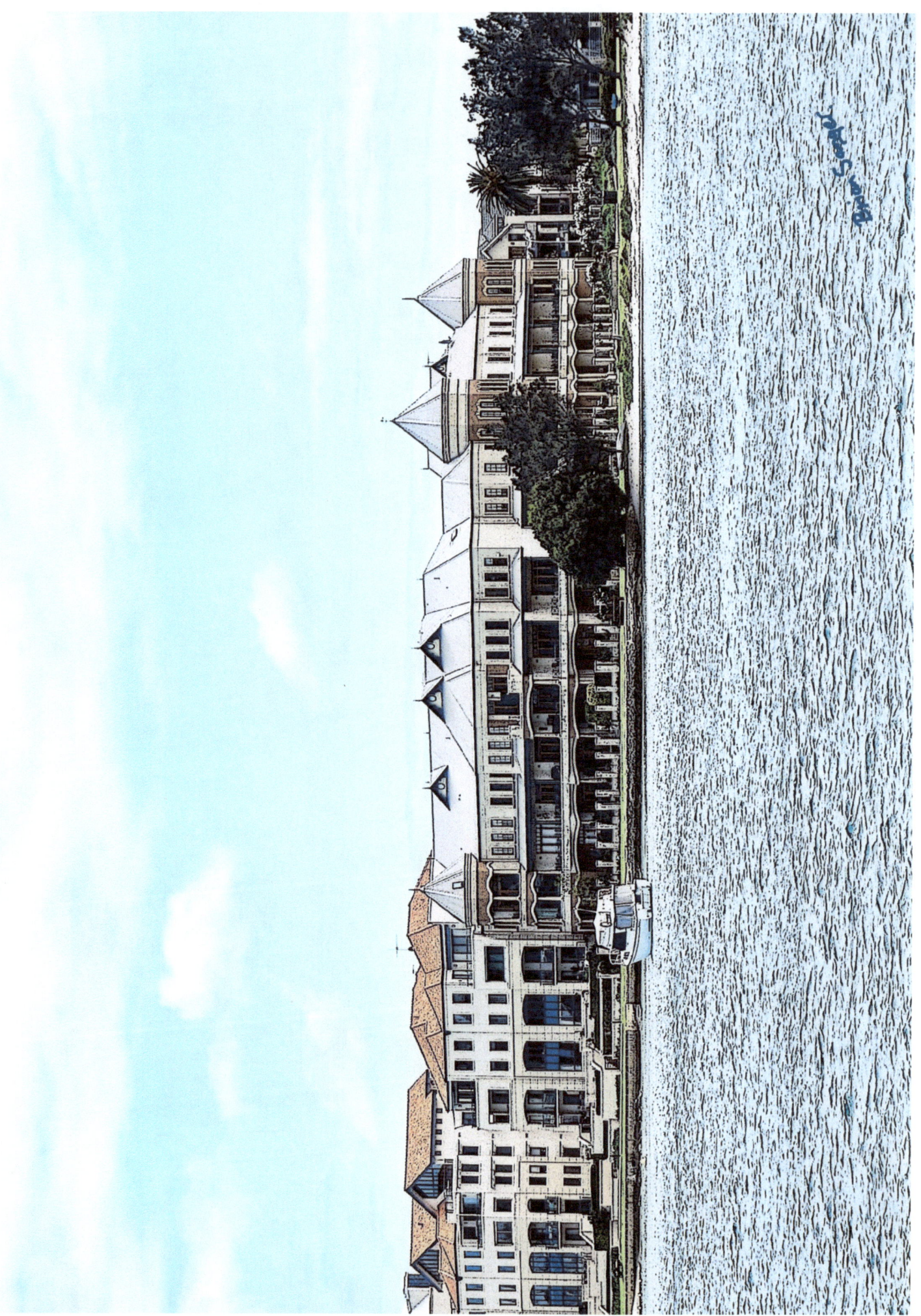

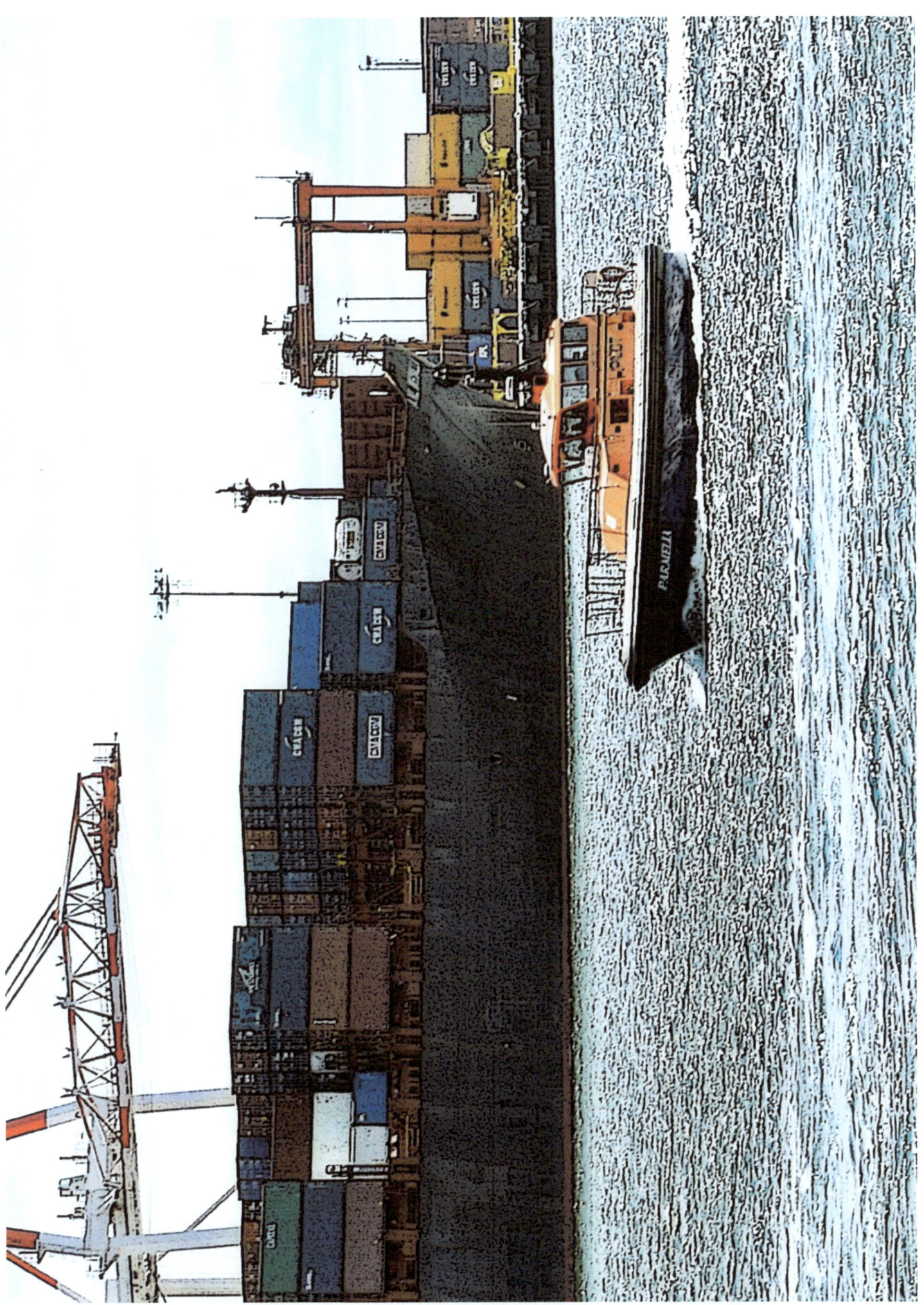

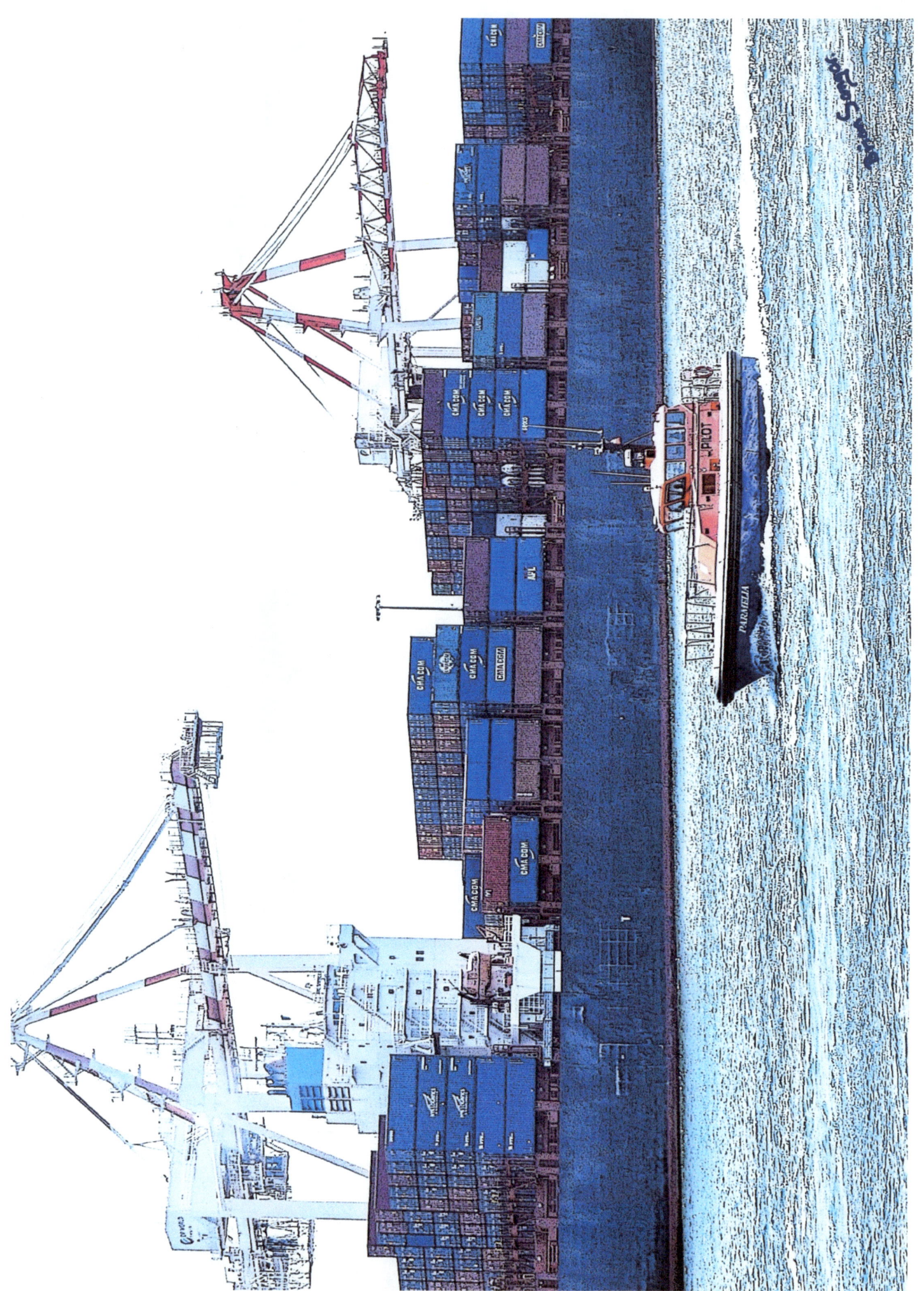

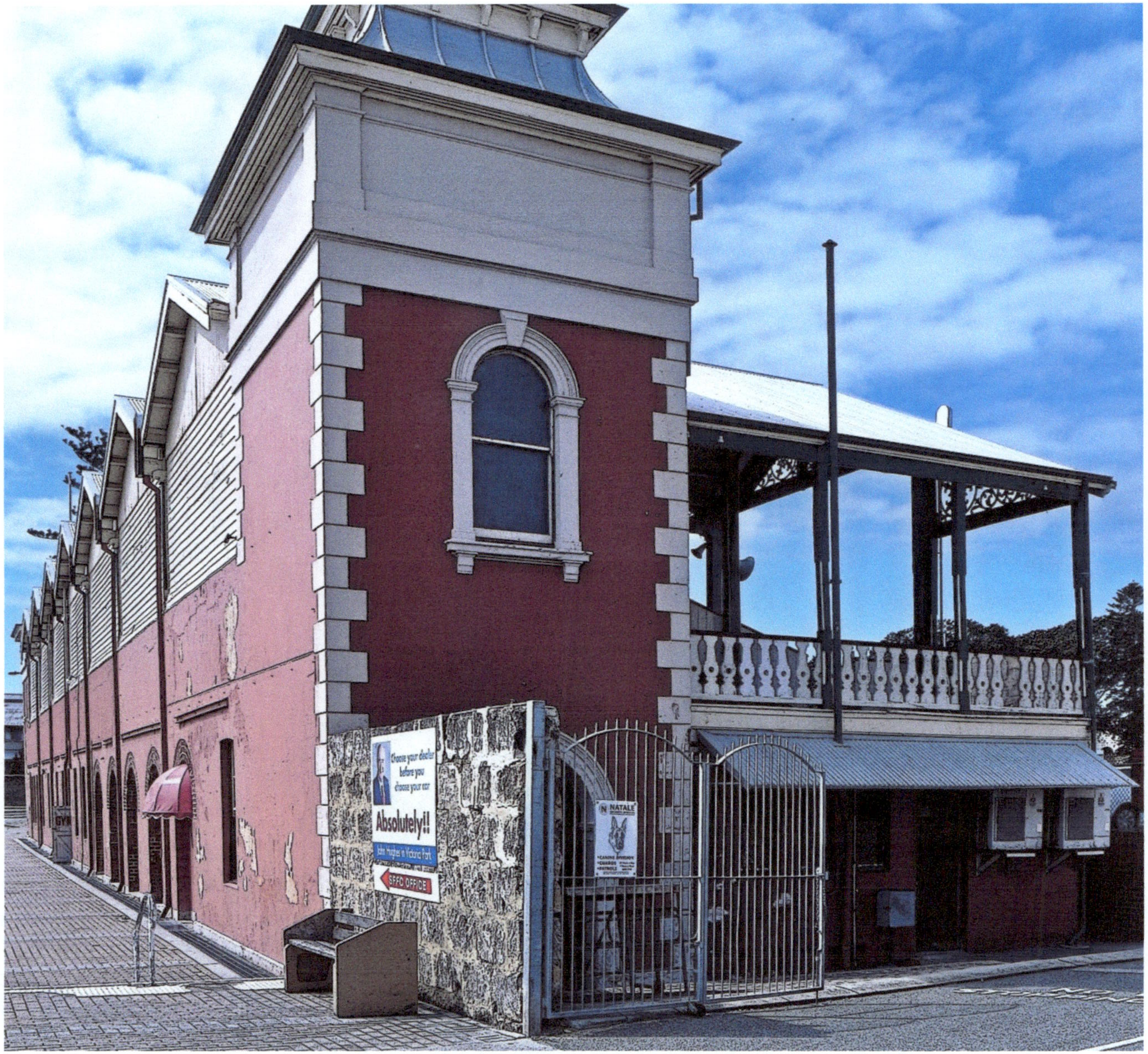

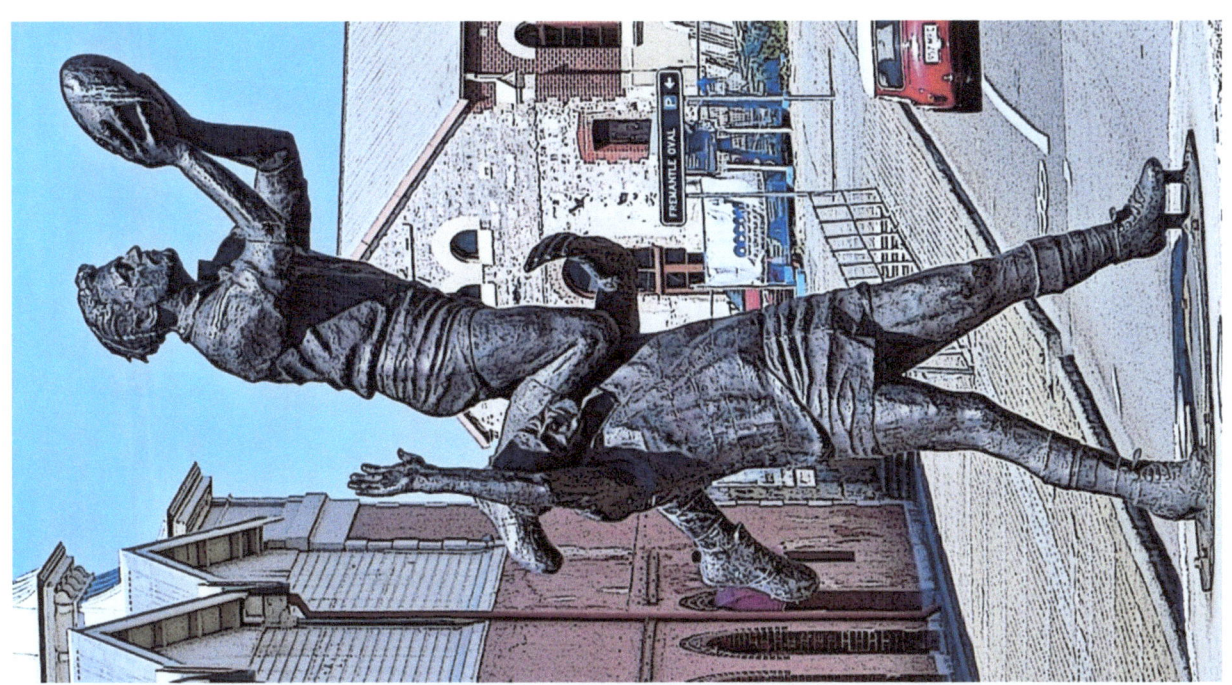

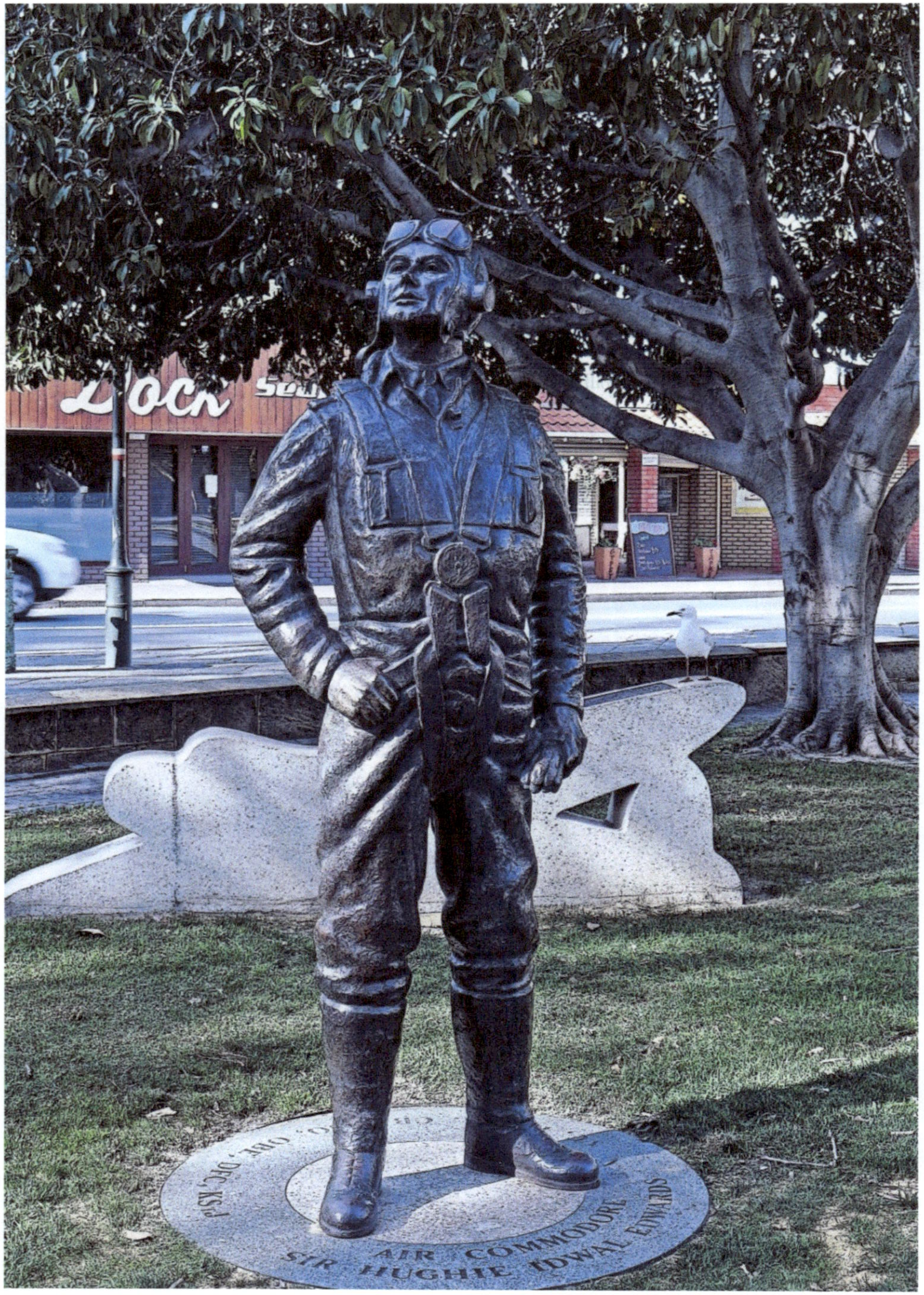

AIR COMMODORE
SIR HUGHIE IDWAL EDWARDS
OBE, DFC, KStJ

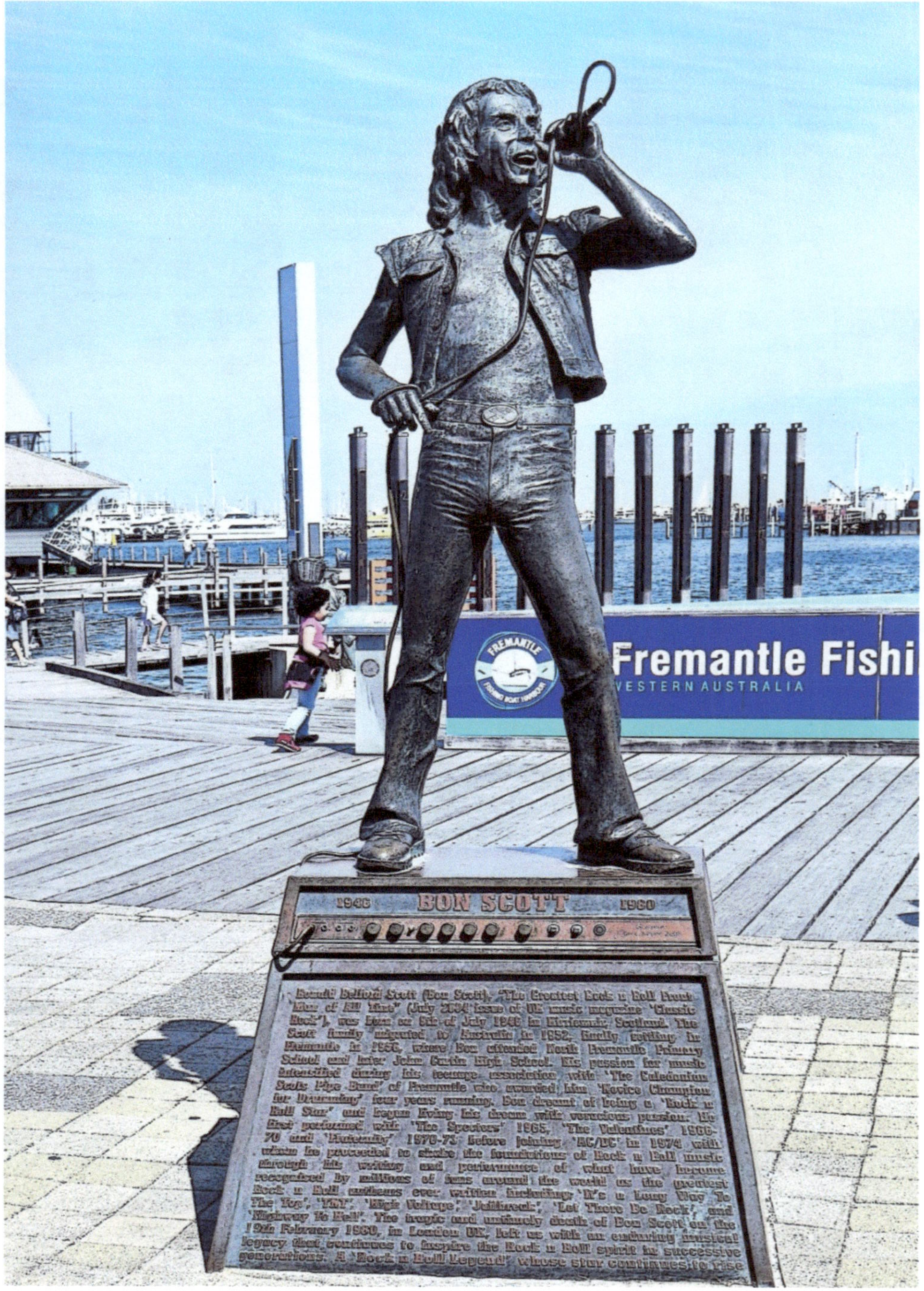

Fremantle Fishi
WESTERN AUSTRALIA
1946 BON SCOTT 1980

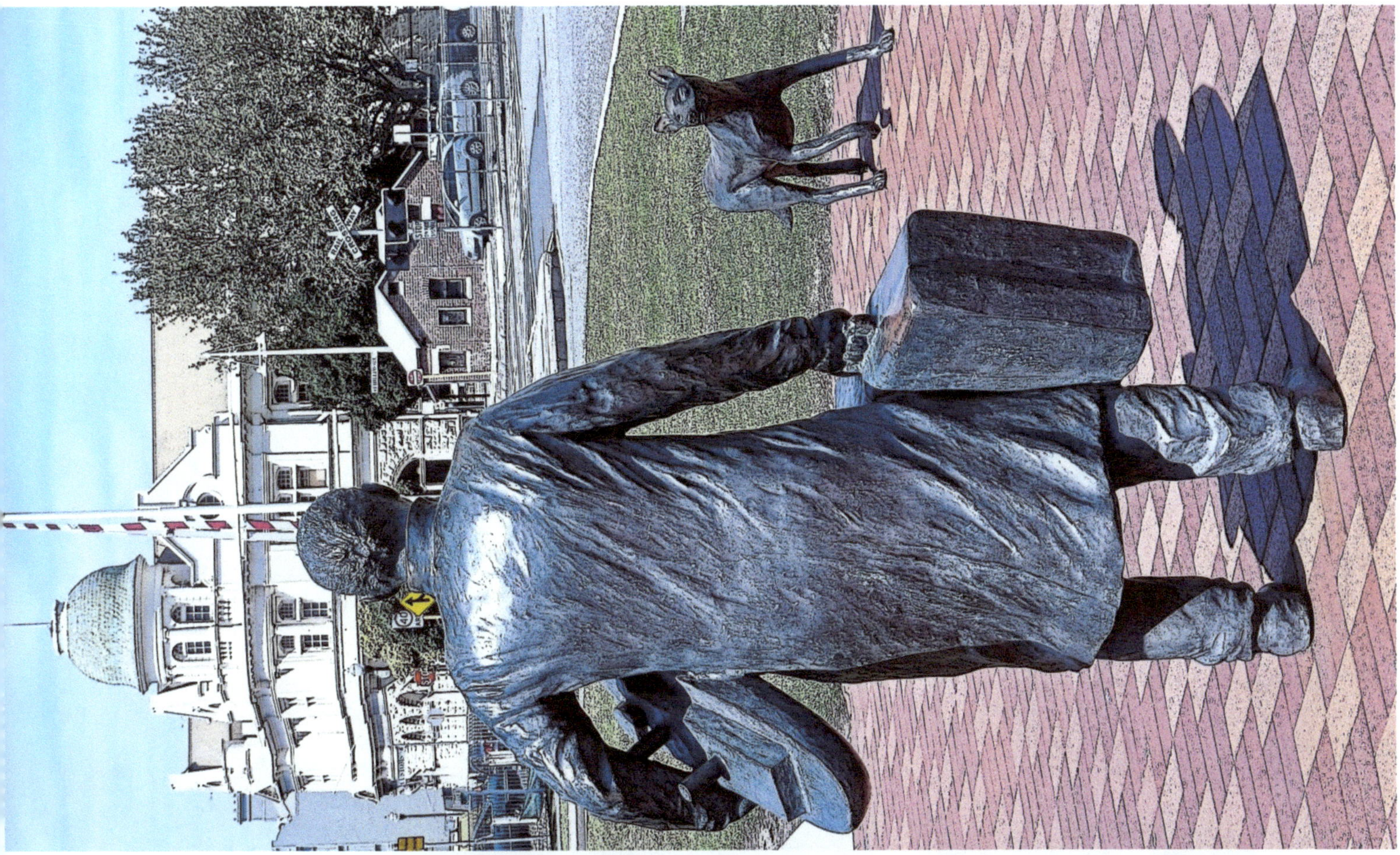

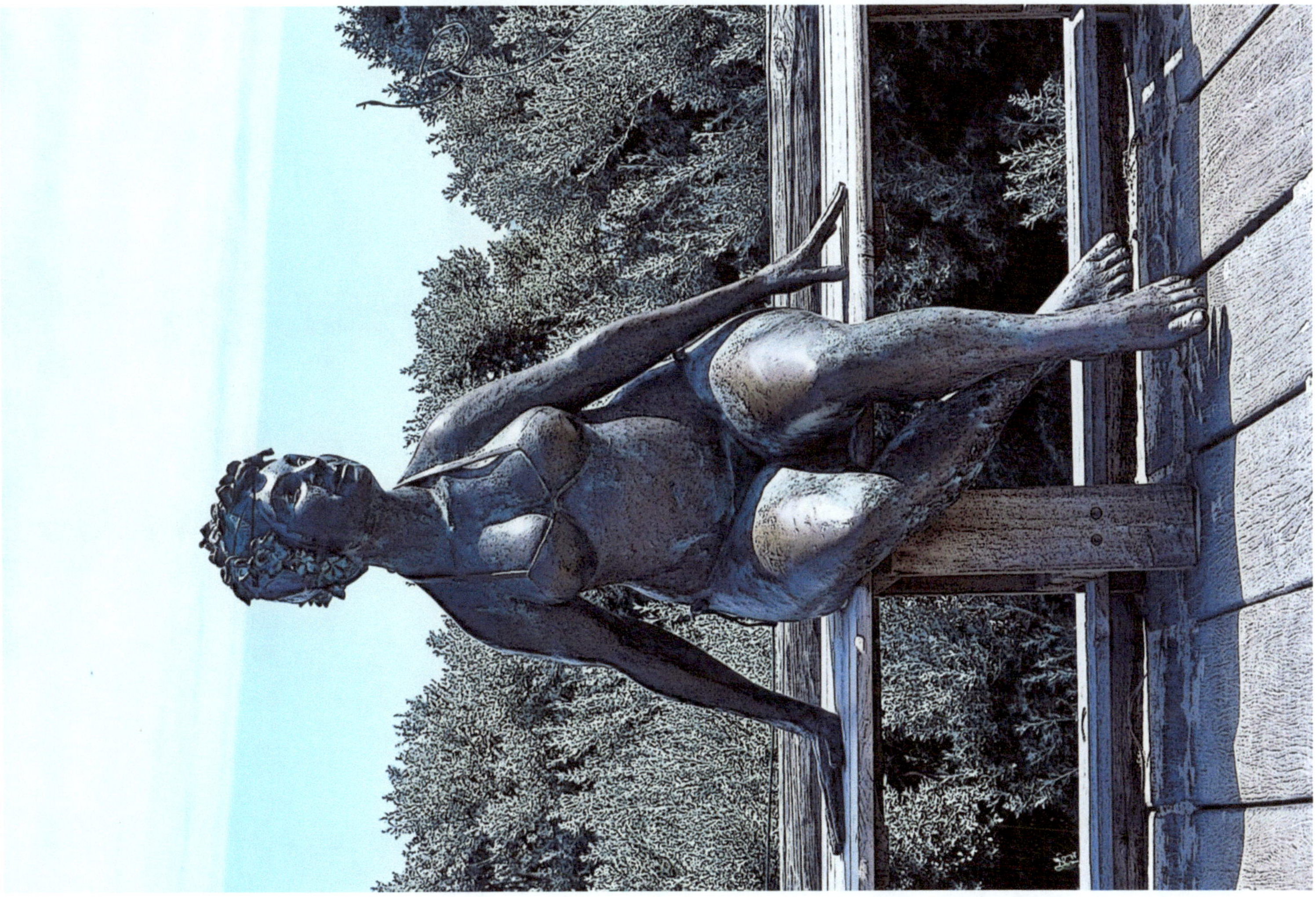

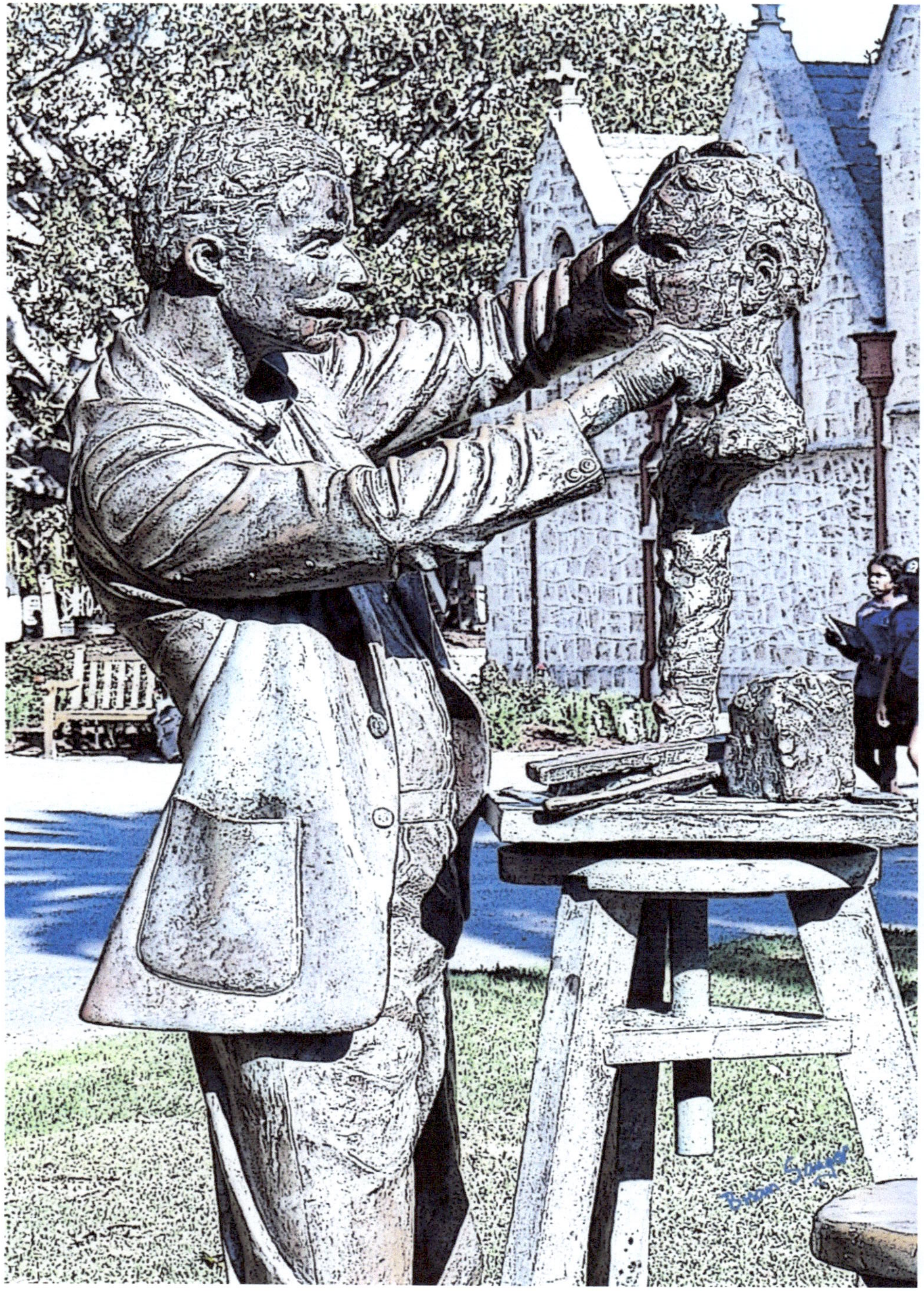

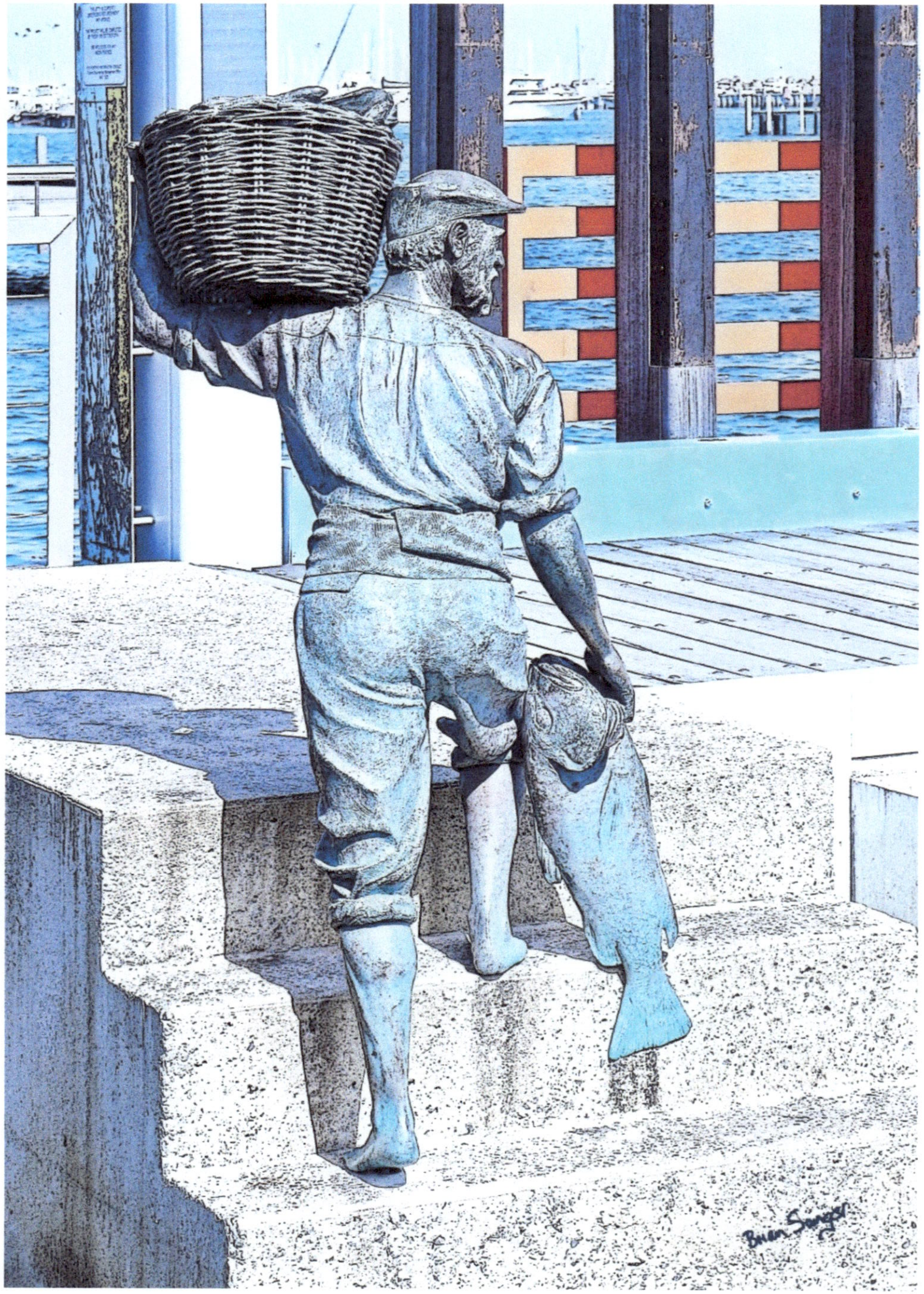

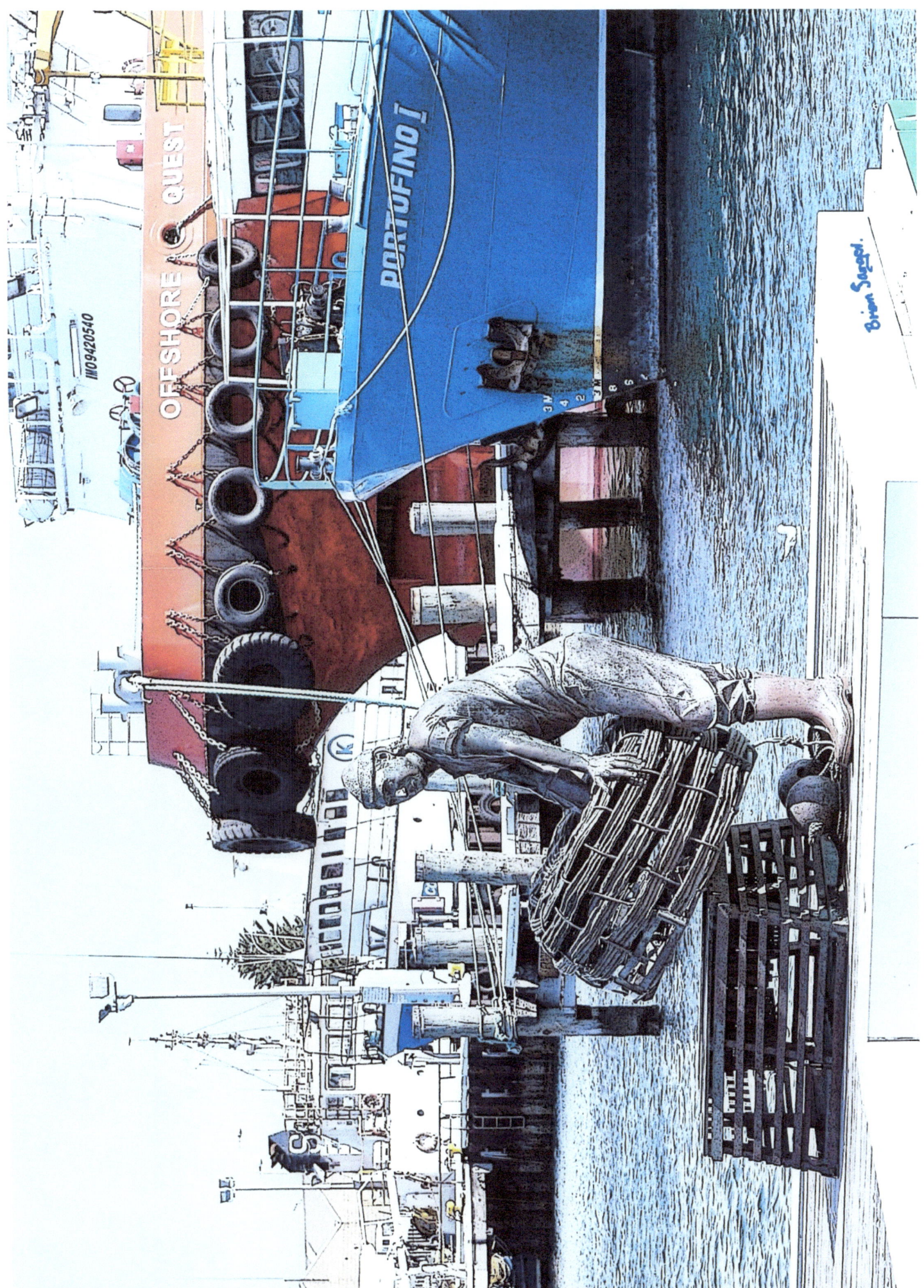

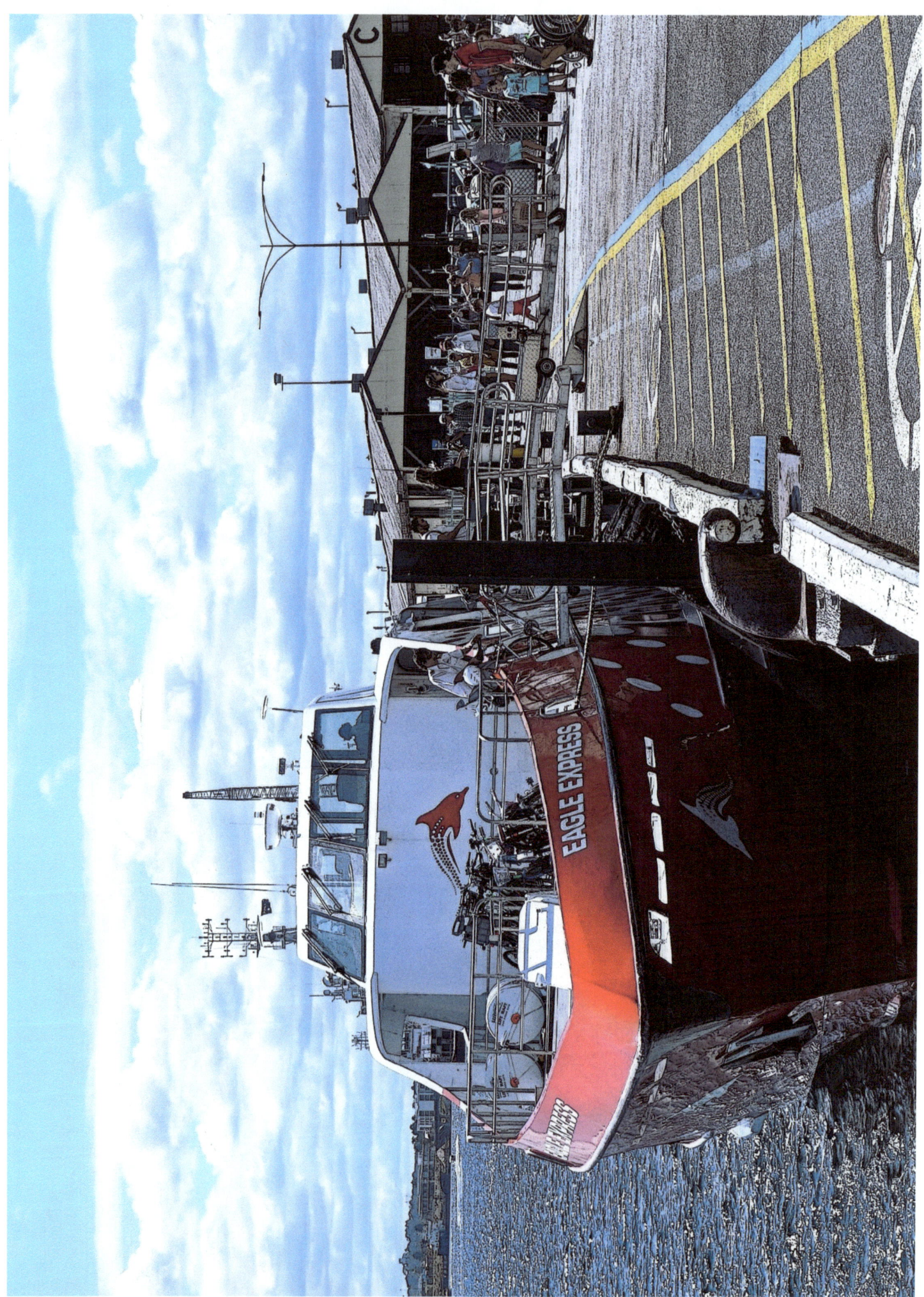

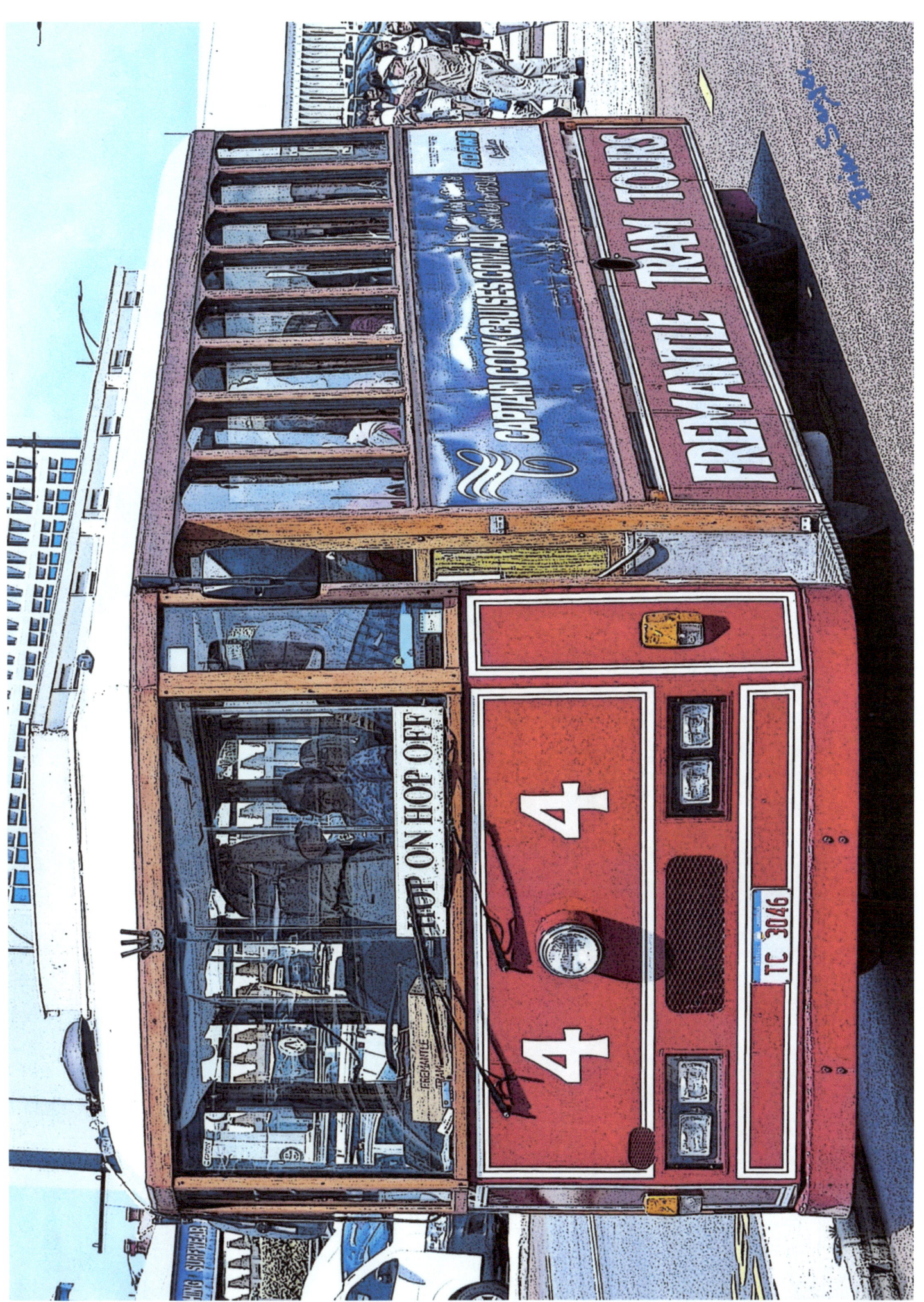

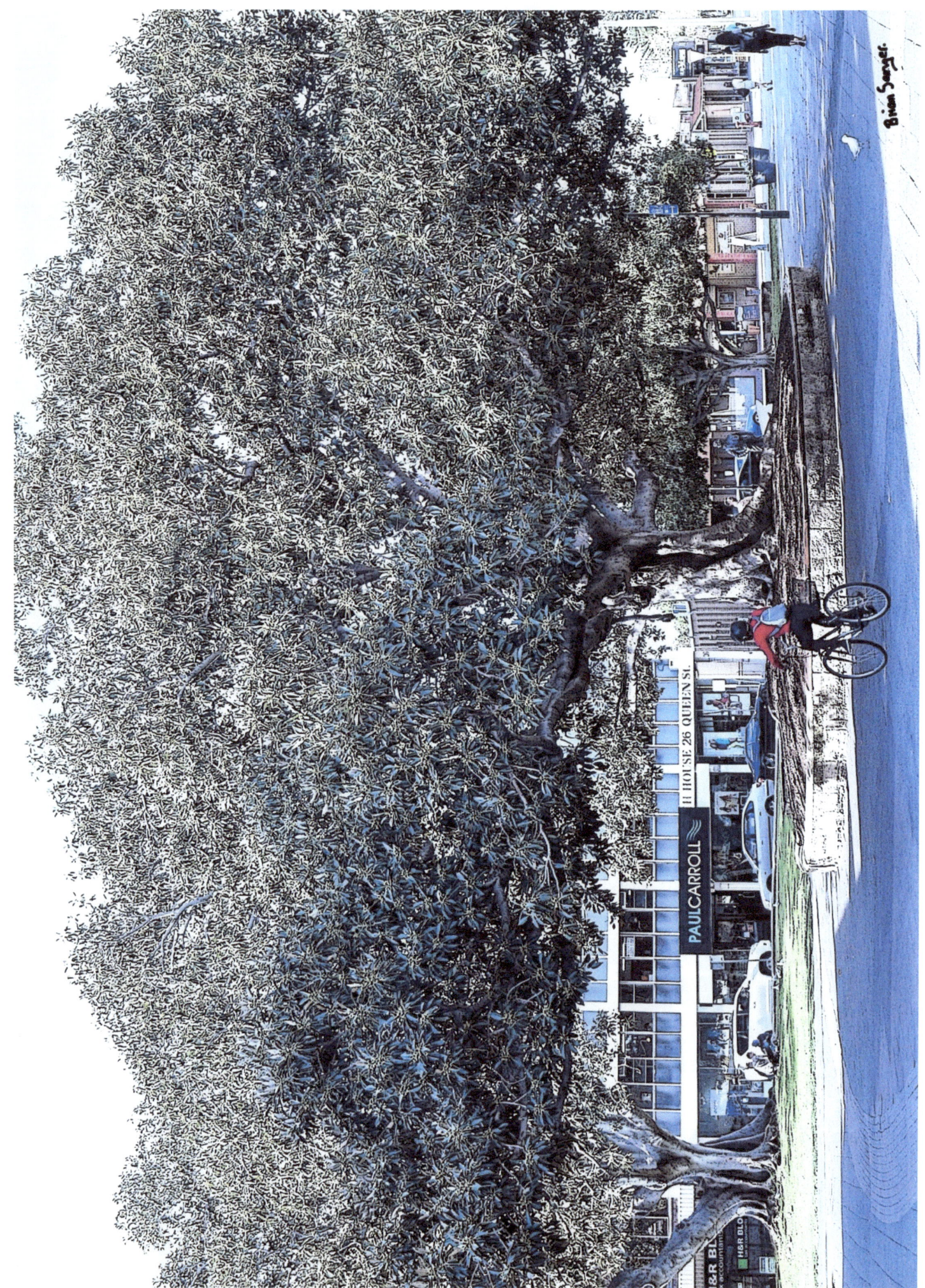

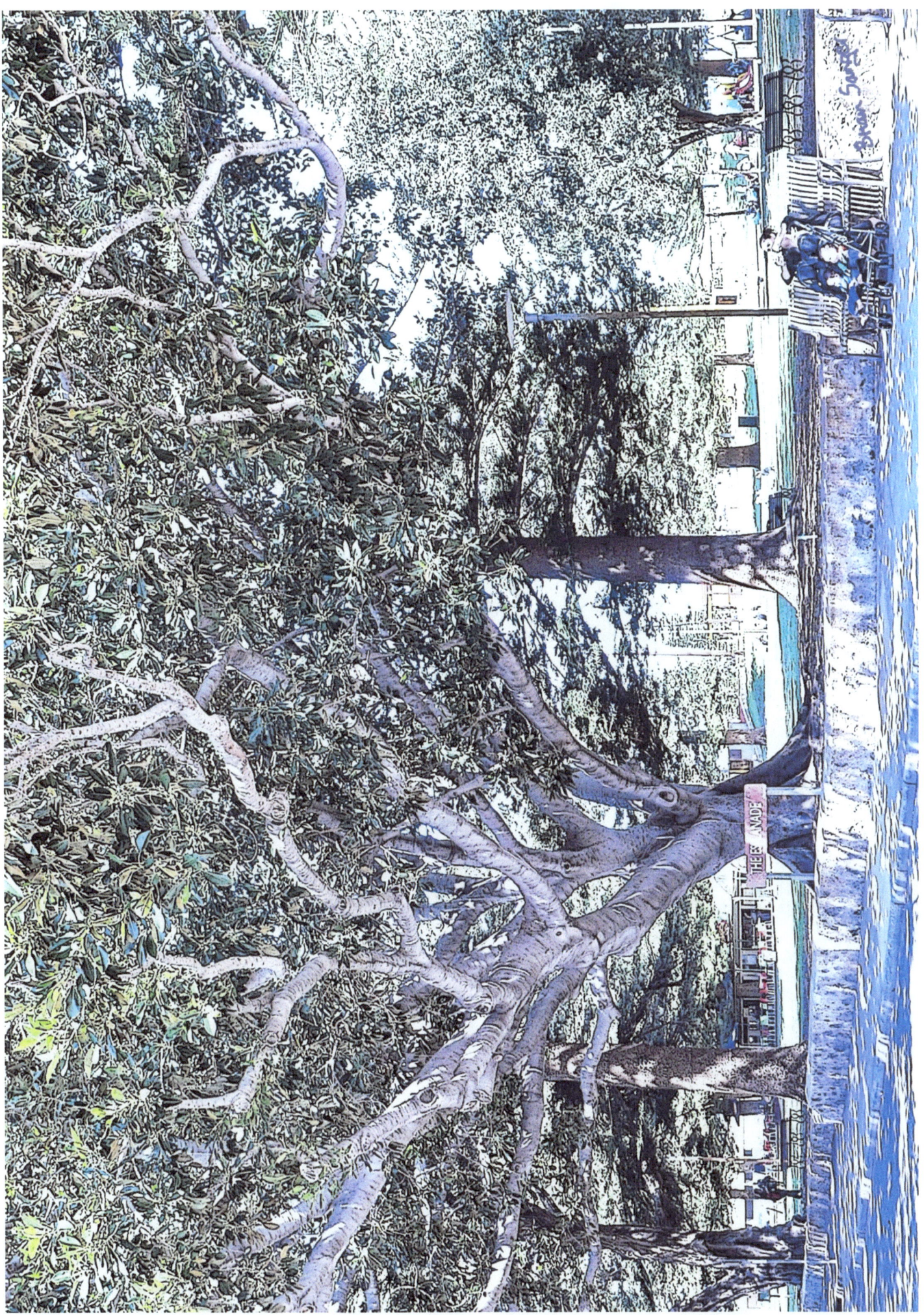

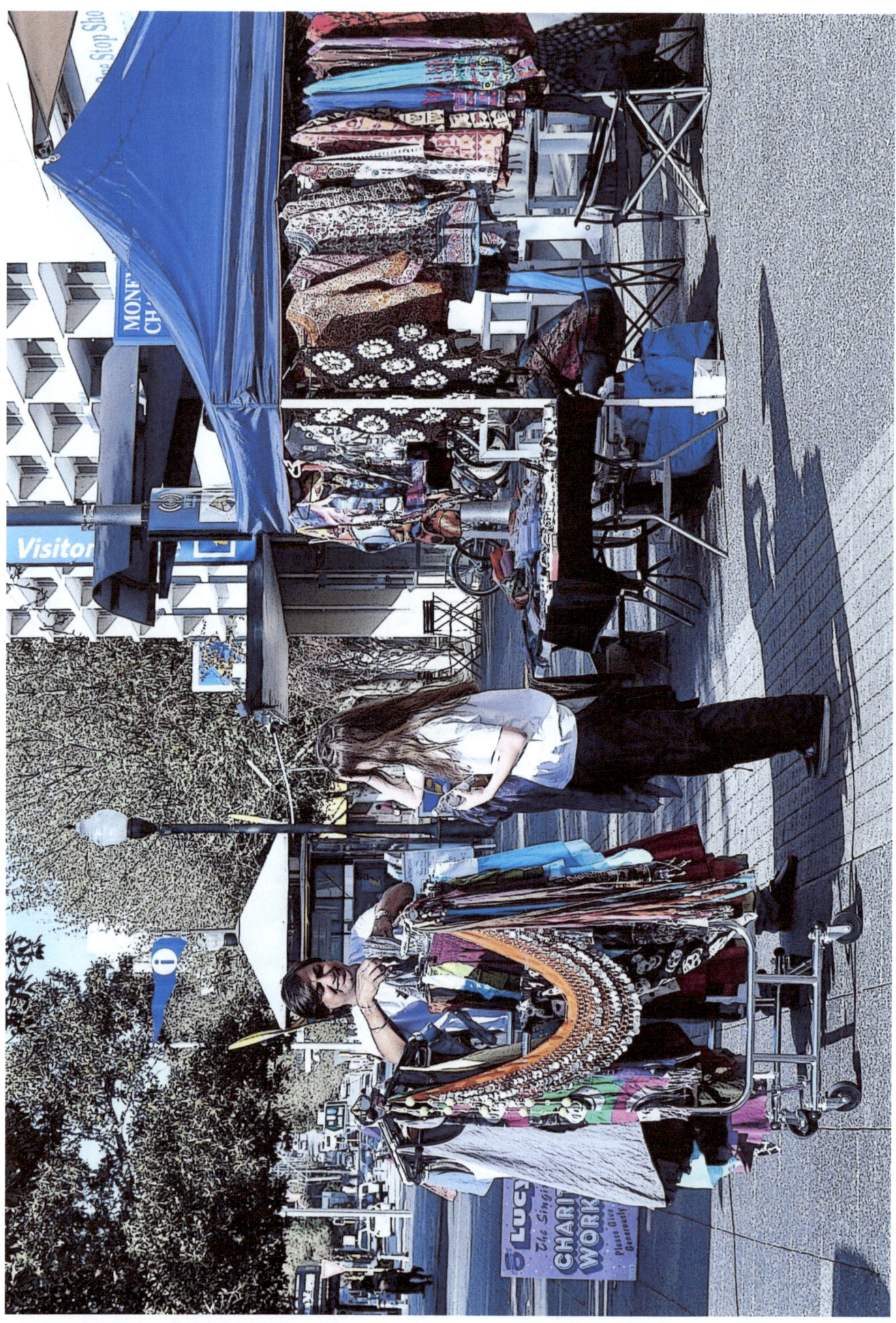

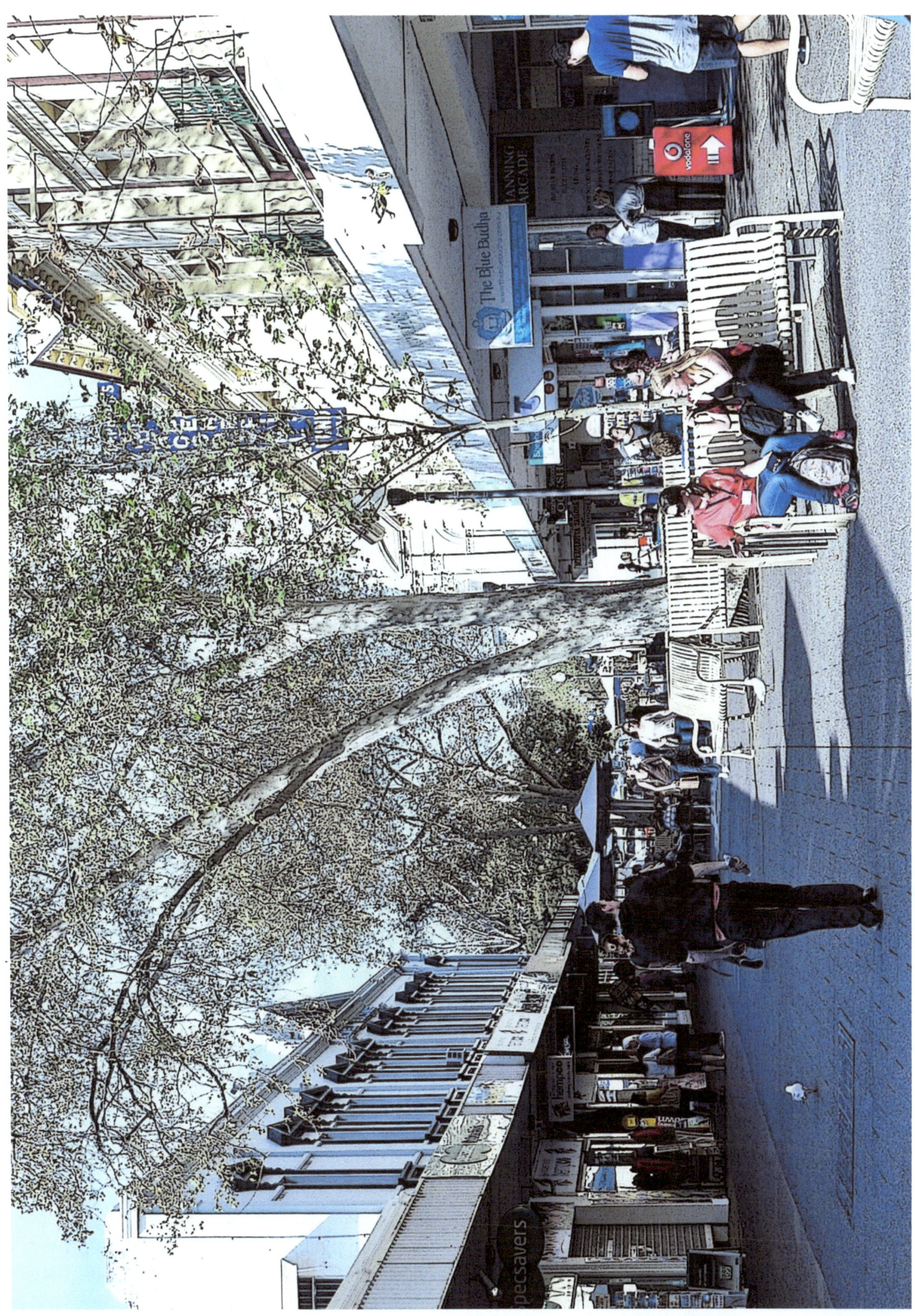

BRIAN SANGER   Photographic Artist

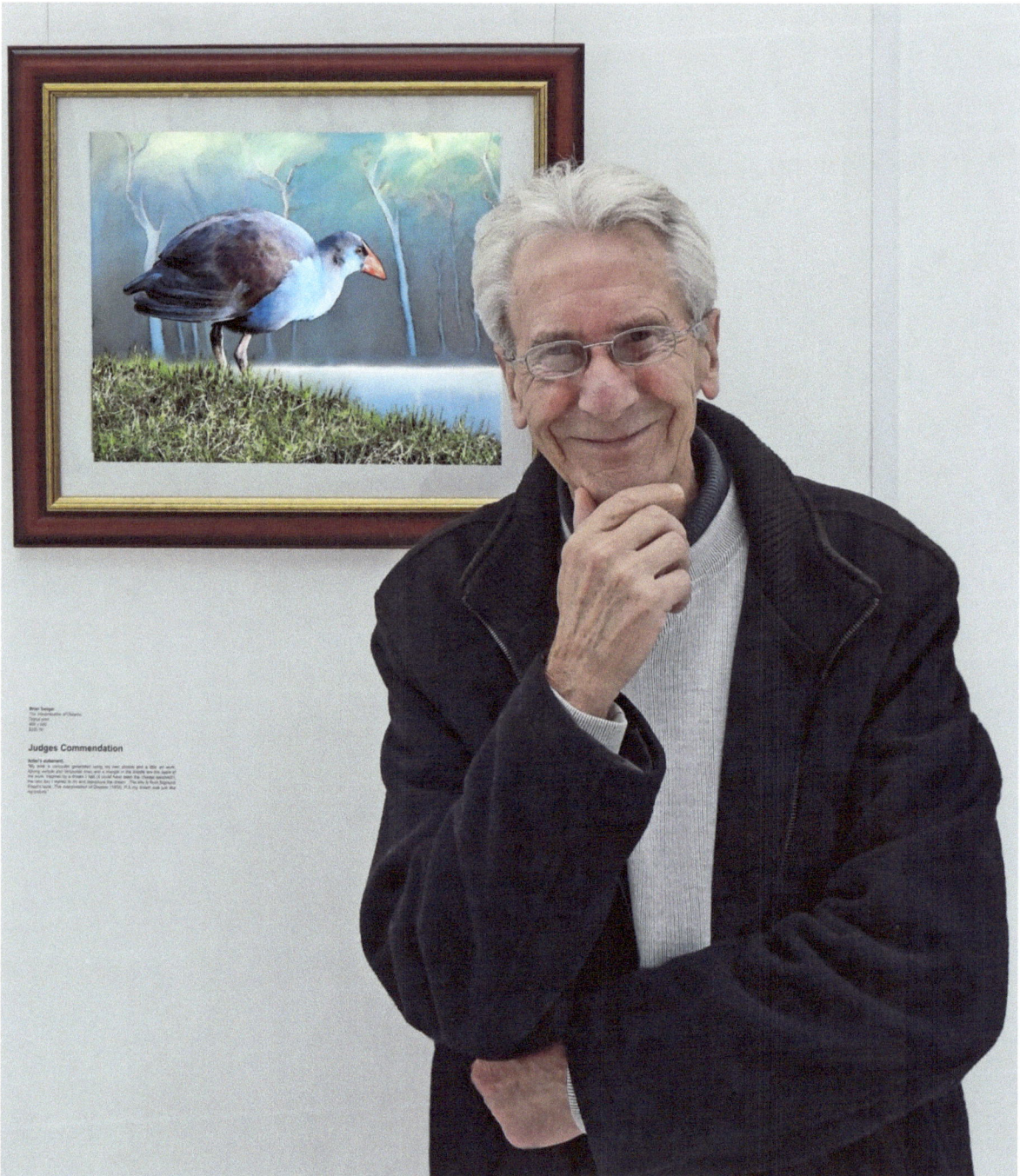

I was born in London in 1939 and remember when I was very young trying to paint a white cat black so it would not stand out during the black outs near the end of the war.

As far as I remember I always liked art. I took art at school but I never had any formal qualifications.

While in my twenties I started taking an interest in photography.

I came to Australia in 1973 with my wife and two young sons and fell in love with the landscape.

Art and photography has been my hobby for many years and even more so since I retired and in the past few years I have taken to combining my photos and art on the computer and my speciality is creating fantasy art and nature working on the computer.